GAO

I0426282

June 2012

DEFENSE MANAGEMENT

Steps Taken to Better Manage Fuel Demand but Additional Information Sharing Mechanisms Are Needed

GAO

Accountability ★ Integrity ★ Reliability

GAO-12-619

Highlights of GAO-12-619, a report to the Chairman, Committee on Armed Services, U.S. Senate

DEFENSE MANAGEMENT

Steps Taken to Better Manage Fuel Demand but Additional Information Sharing Mechanisms Are Needed

Why GAO Did This Study

According to DOD, the U.S. military's dependence on liquid fuel in countries like Afghanistan creates an enormous logistics burden that exposes forces to enemy attack and diverts operational resources from other mission areas to support delivery of this critical resource. In 2011, DOD consumed almost 5 billion gallons of fuel in military operations worldwide, at a cost of approximately $17.3 billion. GAO was asked to (1) assess DOD's approach for fuel demand management, including at forward-deployed locations in Afghanistan, (2) determine the extent to which DOD has initiatives to promote fuel efficiency at forward-deployed locations in Afghanistan and efforts to coordinate and collaborate on such initiatives, and (3) assess efforts to measure the results of its fuel demand management initiatives and establish a baseline measure of fuel consumption in Afghanistan. To conduct this review, GAO analyzed DOD and service guidance and strategies related to fuel demand management and fuel demand management initiatives, visited locations in Afghanistan, and met with DOD officials.

What GAO Recommends

GAO recommends that DOD finalize and implement a systematic approach that includes establishing a mechanism to identify and track fuel demand management initiatives that have been fielded, or are in the research and development phase. DOD partially concurred with GAO's recommendation, citing ongoing efforts to identify and track initiatives. Until fully implemented, GAO is unable to assess whether these efforts fully address the recommendation.

View GAO-12-619. For more information, contact Zina Merritt at (202) 512-5257 or merrittz@gao.gov.

What GAO Found

The Department of Defense (DOD) has taken steps to establish an approach for managing DOD's overall fuel demand, but is still developing comprehensive guidance to address fuel demand management, including at forward-deployed locations in countries such as Afghanistan. In 2009, GAO reported that DOD lacked (1) visibility and accountability for achieving fuel reduction, (2) incentives and a viable funding mechanism to invest in the implementation of fuel demand reduction projects, and (3) guidance and policies that addressed fuel demand at forward-deployed locations. In response to GAO recommendations, DOD has taken steps since 2009 to increase its visibility and accountability for fuel demand management at forward-deployed locations, including those located in Afghanistan. In addition, with an increased focus on fuel demand management, DOD has also provided funding and incentives to implement fuel demand management projects. Further, DOD has issued some guidance on fuel demand management at forward-deployed locations since 2009 and is developing more comprehensive guidance on how DOD will incorporate energy efficiency considerations into operations, planning, and training decisions for current military operations in Afghanistan and for future military operations. DOD's 2012 *Operational Energy Strategy Implementation Plan* acknowledges the need for additional comprehensive guidance and directs the Joint Staff and military departments to report, by the end of fiscal year 2012, on how operational energy considerations will be reflected in policy, doctrine, and professional military education. The Duncan Hunter National Defense Authorization Act for Fiscal Year 2009 requires DOD to report to Congress annually on its progress in implementing its operational energy strategy. DOD has yet to submit its first report.

Multiple DOD organizations are developing initiatives to decrease fuel demand at forward-deployed locations, including in Afghanistan, and the department has worked to facilitate some coordination and collaboration among the services on fuel demand management efforts. However, it is still developing an approach to systematically identify and track all of the fuel demand management initiatives that have been fielded, or are in the research and development phase throughout DOD. GAO's prior work found that utilizing a mechanism such as a database can help organizations enhance their visibility and oversight of DOD programs. Until DOD finalizes its approach to systematically identify and track fuel demand management initiatives, it may be limited in its ability to foster collaboration, achieve efficiencies, and avoid unintended duplication or overlap of activities.

DOD has started to measure the results of some of the fuel demand management initiatives used in Afghanistan, but is still in the process of collecting and assessing comprehensive baseline data needed to measure current fuel consumption at forward-deployed locations. The Army and Marine Corps have begun collecting data on the amount of fuel consumed by their current assets in Afghanistan. Recognizing the need for additional information, DOD's 2012 *Implementation Plan* has tasked the services with developing and refining their fuel consumption baselines by mid-2012 and DOD has provided funding for this purpose. Once collected, these data should enhance DOD's planning, programming, and operational decisions and help DOD assess progress toward meeting its operational energy goals.

_____ **United States Government Accountability Office**

Contents

Table

Figures

United States Government Accountability Office
Washington, DC 20548

June 28, 2012

The Honorable Carl Levin
Chairman
Committee on Armed Services
United States Senate

Dear Mr. Chairman:

The Department of Defense (DOD) depends heavily on petroleum-based fuel to sustain its forward-deployed locations[1] around the world—particularly at remote locations that are not connected to local power grids and must rely on fuel-consuming generators for heating, cooling, lighting, and other base support activities. According to DOD, the U.S. military's dependence on liquid fuel in countries like Afghanistan creates an enormous logistics burden that exposes forces to enemy attack and diverts operational resources from other mission areas to support delivery of this critical resource. In addition, global oil supply routes flow through unstable regions, which can pose supply vulnerabilities, and sharp rises in fuel prices have increased DOD's operating costs at a time when the department faces mandated reductions to defense spending. In 2011, DOD consumed almost 5 billion gallons of fuel in military operations worldwide, at a cost of approximately $17.3 billion. To help reduce its demand for fuel in military activities abroad, the services expect to spend approximately $4 billion over the next 5 years on operational energy initiatives.[2]

Over the past several years, we and others have reported on the challenges DOD faces in managing fuel use at forward-deployed locations, and Congress has required action by DOD on this issue. In February 2008, the Defense Science Board[3] reported that the high

---

[1] For the purposes of this report, we will use the term "forward-deployed locations" to refer to forward operating bases, combat outposts, and other contingency bases occupied by U.S military units.

[2] These initiatives include efforts to reduce the demand for fuel, expand or diversify fuel supplies, and incorporate energy security into the future force. Approximately 58 percent of DOD's funding for operational energy efforts is budgeted for science and technology.

[3] The Defense Science Board is a federal advisory committee established to provide independent advice to the Secretary of Defense.

GAO-12-619 Defense Energy Management

demand for fuel in-theater degrades operational capabilities, exposes support operations to greater risk than necessary, and increases life-cycle costs.[4] In 2009, we reported that each of the services had efforts planned or underway to reduce fuel demand, but these efforts were not well coordinated and DOD lacked an effective approach for implementing its fuel demand management initiatives and maintaining sustained attention to fuel demand management at its forward-deployed locations.[5] The Duncan Hunter National Defense Authorization Act for Fiscal Year 2009 established a Director of Operational Energy Plans and Programs (OEP&P) and developed an operational energy strategy, providing the department with an opportunity to increase attention on improving fuel demand management.[6] As defined in that act, operational energy is energy required for training, moving, and sustaining military forces and weapons platforms for military operations, including tactical power systems, generators, and weapons platforms.[7]

Interested in DOD's progress in addressing these issues since our 2009 report, you asked us to examine DOD's efforts to reduce the demand for and promote the efficient use of fuel by the U.S. military at forward-deployed locations in Afghanistan. Specifically, this report addresses (1) DOD's approach for fuel demand management, including at forward-deployed locations in Afghanistan; (2) the extent to which DOD has initiatives to promote fuel efficiency at forward-deployed locations in Afghanistan and efforts to coordinate and collaborate on such initiatives; and (3) DOD's efforts to measure the results of its fuel demand management initiatives and establish a baseline measure of fuel consumption in Afghanistan.

To address our objectives, we analyzed DOD and military service guidance, relevant legislation, and other documents, and discussed fuel demand issues with agency officials to gain their perspectives on DOD's fuel demand management efforts and challenges. We focused our review

---

[4]Defense Science Board Task Force on DOD Energy Strategy, *More Fight—Less Fuel* (February 2008).

[5]GAO, *Defense Management: DOD Needs to Increase Attention on Fuel Demand Management at Forward-Deployed Locations*, GAO-09-300 (Washington, D.C.: Feb. 20, 2009).

[6]Pub. L. No. 110-417, § 902 (2008).

[7]Pub. L. No. 110-417, § 331 (2008).

on efforts to manage fuel demand to include forward-deployed locations within the Central Command's area of responsibility in Afghanistan.[8] Based on discussions with DOD officials and site visits to forward-deployed locations in Afghanistan, we analyzed the extent to which DOD had established an approach for managing fuel demand at forward-deployed locations and a means to facilitate coordination and collaboration among the services on these initiatives since our 2009 report. Additionally, based on data provided by the services, we identified key fuel demand management initiatives that are currently fielded or are in development and expected to address fuel demand issues at forward-deployed locations. Furthermore, we reviewed strategies the services have in place to measure the results of their fuel demand management initiatives, cost savings data, and the extent to which DOD uses measures to track and assess the results of its initiatives in Afghanistan.

Our review focused on fuel demand management initiatives[9] planned for or underway for use in Afghanistan at contingency bases, referred to as forward-deployed locations throughout our report. Initiatives we reviewed included items such as power generation equipment, soldier systems, and energy efficiency improvements used at land-based forward-deployed locations. To identify fuel demand management initiatives planned for or currently in use in Afghanistan, we queried OEP&P, the services, and DOD organizations involved in operational energy research and development. Based on the information provided, we identified over 30 fuel demand management initiatives. After consultation with Central Command and U.S. Forces-Afghanistan officials, we selected and visited the following forward-deployed locations in Afghanistan to gain a firsthand understanding of fuel demand reduction efforts and any implementation challenges: Bagram Airfield, Camp Leatherneck, Camp Phoenix, Camp Sabalu-Harrison, Joint Combat Outpost Pul-A-Sayed, the New Kabul Compound, and Patrol Base Boldak. We chose to visit these locations because they were using energy-efficient technologies that were included

---

[8]There are six geographic combatant commands: Africa Command, Central Command, European Command, Northern Command, Pacific Command, and Southern Command.

[9]For the purposes of this report, the term fuel demand management initiatives includes nonmateriel and materiel solutions to assist DOD in reducing its reliance on fuel consumed at forward-deployed locations. Nonmateriel solutions include efforts such as changes to policies and procedures, or modifications to staffing to perform fuel demand management functions. Materiel solutions include developing equipment such as more efficient generators or environmental control units.

in our review and/or are illustrative of DOD's fuel demand management initiatives and challenges. We concentrated our review on the steps the Army and Marine Corps have taken to reduce fuel demand because these two services have the responsibility for managing forward-deployed locations in Afghanistan.

We conducted this performance audit from April 2011 to June 2012 in accordance with generally accepted government auditing standards. Those standards require that we plan and perform the audit to obtain sufficient, appropriate evidence to provide a reasonable basis for our findings and conclusions based on our audit objectives. We believe that the evidence obtained provides a reasonable basis for our findings and conclusions based on our audit objectives. Details about our scope and methodology are contained in appendix I.

Background

DOD's Forward-Deployed Locations in Afghanistan

At any given time, the United States has military personnel serving abroad in forward-deployed locations to support U.S. strategic interests. The number of personnel and locations vary with the frequency and type of military operations and deployment demands. In general, operational control of U.S. military forces at forward-deployed locations is assigned to the nation's six geographic, unified overseas regional commands, including Central Command.[10] Central Command's area of responsibility includes Afghanistan, where military operations have led to the creation of several hundred locations that vary in size and structure to meet mission requirements, and the military service components have been responsible for establishing and maintaining these locations. Some forward operating bases such as Bagram Air Field support thousands of personnel and are large consumers of energy. Forward operating bases generally support a brigade[11] or larger population and are typically composed of temporary or semi-permanent structures that require energy for lighting, heating, and air conditioning; electrical power grids; water and sewage systems; and

---

[10]U.S. Transportation Command and U.S. Special Operations Command frequently retain operational control over their respective forces when deployed.

[11]A brigade ranges in size from about 1,500-3,200 military personnel. A company generally consists of 60-200 personnel.

GAO-12-619 Defense Energy Management

force protection systems. At the other end of the spectrum, small units at the company level and below have established combat outposts to enhance local operations. These outposts have a short life-cycle and unique configurations. Since these forward-deployed locations can be constructed in a variety of ways, the amount of fuel they consume can vary. Figure 1 shows the forward-deployed locations we visited during the course of our review.

Figure 1: Forward-Deployed Locations in Afghanistan Visited during GAO's Review of DOD's Fuel Demand Management Efforts

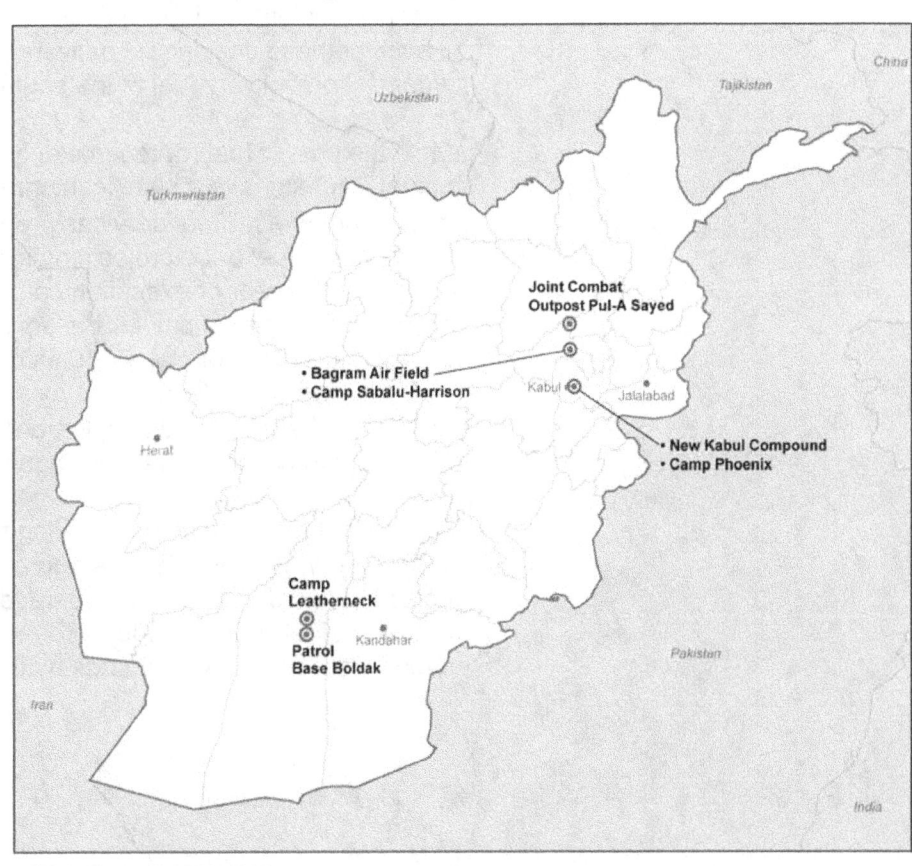

Sources: GAO; Map Resources (map).

DOD Fuel Demand, Delivery Responsibilities, and Costs

Military deployments generally rely on petroleum-based fuels, which power communication equipment, expeditionary bases, tactical vehicles, aircraft, some naval vessels, and other platforms. According to DOD officials, more than 43 million gallons of fuel, on average, were supplied each month to support U.S. forces in Afghanistan in 2011.[12] Equipment such as generators provides power for base support activities such as air conditioning, heating, lighting, and communications, and consumes a significant amount of fuel

In Afghanistan, the Defense Logistics Agency-Energy (DLA-Energy) delivers fuel to multiple points of delivery throughout the country via contracted trucking assets, depending on the location of the bases. DLA-Energy tracks the aggregate amount of fuel the services consume based on sales receipts, and the U.S. government pays for fuel that is delivered to each of these designated delivery points. The North Atlantic Treaty Organization delivers fuel in the southern part of Afghanistan.

While the cost of fuel represents only about 2 percent of DOD's total budget,[13] it can have a significant impact on the department's operating costs. Since the military services prepare their annual budgets based on the approved fuel price projections in the President's budget, market volatility in the year of execution can result in out-of-cycle fuel price increases that are difficult for the services to absorb. A prior DOD report has estimated that for every $10 increase in the price of a barrel of oil, DOD's operating costs increase by approximately $1.3 billion.[14] The department has received supplemental appropriations from Congress in prior years to cover budget shortages associated with rising fuel prices.

Moreover, the total cost of delivering fuel to a consumer on the battlefield—which includes the aggregate cost of buying, moving, and protecting fuel during combat operations—can be much greater than the cost of the fuel itself. A 2008 Defense Science Board task force report noted that preliminary estimates by the OSD Program Analysis and

---

[12]This figure includes the quantity of fuel supplied to U.S. forces by DOD and North Atlantic Treaty Organization's Joint Forces Command-Brunssum in its area of operations.

[13]The defense budget in fiscal year 2012 was approximately $646 billion, of which $14.8 billion was requested to fund DOD's fuel requirements.

[14]Defense Science Board Task Force on DOD Energy Strategy, *More Fight—Less Fuel* (February 2008).

Evaluation office[15] and the Institute for Defense Analyses showed that the fully burdened cost[16] of a $2.50 gallon of fuel (DLA's standard price for fuel in 2008) [17] begins at about $15, not including force protection requirements for supply convoys. In addition, fuel delivered in-flight was estimated to cost about $42 a gallon at that time. However, the report notes that these figures were considered low when the report was published in 2008 and, according to DOD officials, in 2011, the cost of a gallon of this fuel had risen to $3.95 (DLA standard price in 2011), making the fully burdened cost of fuel even higher than previously reported. In fiscal year 2009 Congress required the Secretary of Defense to incorporate the fully burdened cost of fuel into its cost analyses, including acquisition analyses of alternatives and program design trade decisions.[18] At the time of our review, DOD officials stated the department was in the process of analyzing the fully burdened cost of fuel and how it will be applied throughout DOD's acquisition process.

DOD Has Taken Steps to Establish an Approach for Fuel Demand Management, but Is Still Developing Comprehensive Guidance

DOD has taken steps since our 2009 report to establish an approach for managing overall fuel demand, but is still developing comprehensive guidance to address fuel demand management. In 2009, we reported that DOD faced difficulty in reducing its reliance on fuel at forward-deployed locations because managing fuel demand had not been a departmental priority and its fuel reduction efforts had not been well coordinated or comprehensive. As such, we recommended that DOD develop requirements for managing fuel demand at forward-deployed locations, and DOD concurred with this recommendation. Since that time, DOD has taken several steps to increase its visibility and accountability for fuel demand management, and is developing comprehensive guidance on how DOD will incorporate energy efficiency considerations into

---

[15]The Weapon Systems Acquisition Reform Act of 2009, Pub. L. 111-23, established a Director of Cost Assessment and Performance Evaluation, who is responsible for ensuring that cost estimates are fair, reliable, and unbiased, and for performing the program analysis and evaluation functions previously performed by the Director of Program Analysis and Evaluation.

[16]Fully burdened cost is defined as the commodity price for fuel plus the total cost of all personnel and assets required to move and, when necessary, protect the fuel from the point at which the fuel is received from the commercial supplier to the point of use.

[17]This is the standard price for JP-8, a fuel used in U.S. military aircraft, vehicles, and other equipment.

[18]Pub. L. 110-417, § 332(c).

operations, planning, and training decisions for current and future military operations.

Progress in Establishing Visibility and Accountability for Overall DOD Fuel Demand Management

DOD has made progress in establishing visibility and accountability for fuel demand management since our 2009 report by making organizational changes and issuing an *Operational Energy Strategy* (operational energy strategy)[19] and related *Operational Energy Strategy Implementation Plan* (implementation plan)[20] to provide direction for DOD's overall fuel demand management efforts, including efforts at forward-deployed locations in Afghanistan. Specifically, in our prior report we noted that DOD's organizational framework did not provide the department with visibility or accountability over fuel demand management issues at forward-deployed locations because there was no one office or official specifically responsible for these issues. We also found that fuel demand reduction efforts were not consistently shared across DOD. Our prior work has shown that visibility and accountability for results are established by assigning roles and responsibilities, establishing goals and metrics, and monitoring performance.

Congress and DOD have taken multiple steps to address this issue. For instance, the Duncan Hunter National Defense Authorization Act for Fiscal Year 2009 established a Director of Operational Energy Plans and Programs (OEP&P)[21] responsible for serving as the principal advisor to the Secretary of Defense for operational energy plans and programs, which includes, among other responsibilities, monitoring and reviewing all operational energy initiatives in DOD. Since its establishment, OEP&P has worked in conjunction with all of the services' energy offices to provide visibility and accountability for operational energy issues, including fuel demand management issues. For example, with input from the services, OEP&P published the *Operational Energy Strategy Implementation Plan* in March 2012 that assigns responsibilities for key tasks and specifies milestones and reporting requirements that will provide accountability for implementing the operational energy strategy

---

[19] *DOD Operational Energy Strategy, Energy for the Warfighter*, May 2011.

[20] *Operational Energy Strategy Implementation Plan*, Department of Defense, March 2012.

[21] In 2011, Congress redesignated the Director of Operational Energy Plans and Programs as the Assistant Secretary of Defense for Operational Energy Plans and Programs. Pub. L. No. 111-383, § 901(a)(1)(B).

(see appendix II). Also, in March 2012, DOD established a Defense Operational Energy Board to help provide visibility and accountability over operational energy efforts that included fuel demand management. The board will be cochaired by the Assistant Secretary of Defense for Operational Energy Plans and Programs and the Joint Staff's Director of Logistics. According to OEP&P officials, the board will help review, synchronize, and support departmentwide operational energy policies, plans, and programs. In addition, the board will monitor and, where necessary, recommend revisions to DOD policies, plans, and programs needed to implement the operational energy strategy. DOD's operational energy strategy, the implementation plan, and the Defense Operational Energy Board are intended to support departmentwide operational energy efforts while also having a direct impact on DOD's efforts to manage fuel demand at forward-deployed locations in Afghanistan. Figure 2 provides a timeline of key events in OEP&P's efforts to manage operational energy issues.

Figure 2: Timeline of Key Events in OEP&P's Efforts to Manage Operational Energy Issues

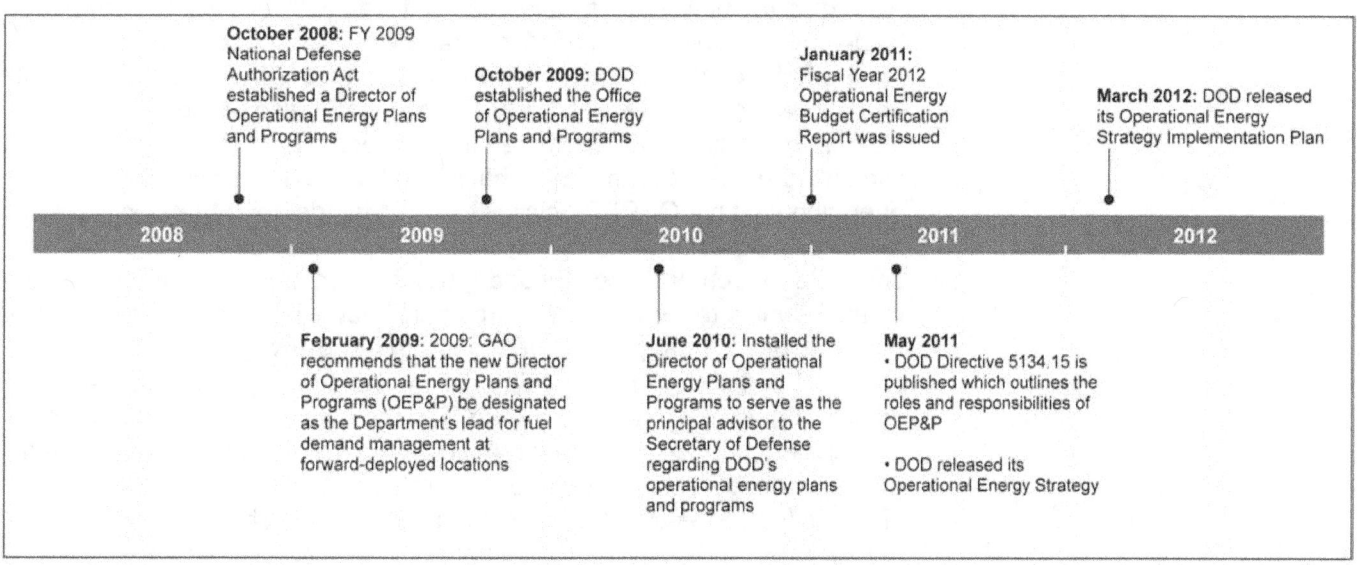

Source: GAO analysis.

To further enhance DOD's operational energy efforts, the National Defense Authorization Act for Fiscal Year 2012 required the Chairman of the Joint Chiefs of Staff to designate a senior official under the jurisdiction of the Chairman to be responsible for operational energy plans and programs.[22] In August 2011, the Chairman appointed the Joint Staff's Director of Logistics to this position with responsibility for coordinating with OEP&P and implementing initiatives pursuant to the operational energy strategy. According to Joint Staff officials, the Joint Staff is committed to addressing operational energy capability gaps and in April 2012 formed a Joint Capabilities Task Group to identify and address fuel demand management issues. The task group's mission includes:

- providing recommendations to better integrate operational energy into current and future materiel and nonmateriel solutions to improve operational capabilities, and
- supporting evaluation of the operational energy requirements process, and providing recommendations through the requisite Functional Capabilities Boards and the Joint Logistics Board to the Joint Capabilities Board or Joint Requirements Oversight Council for validation/decision.

According to Joint Staff officials, the Joint Capabilities Task Group will focus on developing a framework for analysis that supports service and DOD efforts to inform leaders such as commanders in Afghanistan about operational energy vulnerabilities. The group will also propose guidance to support the combatant commands in assessing logistics plans and evaluating energy assumptions that will influence the execution of operational plans. OEP&P officials told us that the Joint Staff plays a key role in collaborating with OSD to create policy, develop joint doctrine, and advocate for combatant commander requirements. Joint Staff officials told us their goal is to incorporate energy efficiency guidance into existing joint publications when such documents are up for review.[23] As part of this process the Joint Staff's Joint Capabilities Task Group will prioritize which guidance documents will be revised first, then work toward updating other applicable guidance documents. According to DOD officials, when these guidance documents are updated, operational energy issues, including priorities for addressing fuel demand management, should be included in the services' and combatant commanders' mission planning activities.

---

[22]Pub. L. No. 112-81, § 311.

[23]According to Joint Staff officials, guidance documents such as Joint Publications should be reviewed and updated every 3 years.

Our prior work on government performance and management also notes the importance of establishing goals and metrics to assess progress and provide accountability.[24] DOD's operational energy strategy established three overarching operational energy goals to: (1) reduce demand for energy in military operations, (2) expand and secure energy supplies, and (3) build energy security into the future force, and DOD has begun to take steps to establish metrics to measure progress toward these goals. OEP&P officials told us that the Defense Operational Energy Board will develop departmental operational energy performance metrics to promote the energy efficiency of military operations by the end of fiscal year 2012. The board will also monitor and, as needed, recommend revisions to DOD policies needed to implement the operational energy strategy and monitor progress to ensure DOD is meeting its operational energy goals. OEP&P officials stated that establishing such strategies, goals, and metrics will not only provide DOD with the direction and tools needed to assess progress towards meeting fuel demand management goals at forward-deployed locations, including those in Afghanistan, but will enhance DOD's efforts to achieve its overall fuel demand management objectives worldwide.

DOD Funding and Incentives for Fuel Demand Management at Forward-deployed Locations

Since our 2009 report, DOD has taken action to fund fuel demand management initiatives and restructure maintenance contract task orders to include energy efficiency considerations and incentives. In our 2009 report on fuel demand management, we found that DOD had not established incentives or a viable funding mechanism for fuel reduction projects at forward-deployed locations and commanders were not encouraged to identify fuel reduction projects as a priority. Specifically, we found that much of the funding provided to support military operations in Iraq and Afghanistan was provided through supplemental funding measures,[25] making it difficult to plan for and fund costly projects such as fuel demand management initiatives. As such, we recommended that DOD establish incentives for commanders of forward-deployed locations to promote fuel demand reduction at their locations, as well as identify a

---

[24]GAO, *Executive Guide: Effectively Implementing the Government Performance and Results Act,* GAO/GGD-96-118 (Washington, D.C.: June 1996).

[25]Supplemental appropriations provide additional budget authority for unanticipated activities or requirements too urgent to be delayed until the regular appropriation is enacted.

viable funding mechanism for the department and commanders of forward-deployed locations to pursue fuel reduction initiatives. DOD partially concurred with our recommendation and said it was not convinced that financial incentives represent the best fuel reduction strategy for forward-deployed locations, but stated that it will seek to incorporate fuel reduction incentives while recognizing the primacy of mission accomplishment. Since the release of our 2009 report, DOD's increased focus on fuel demand management at forward-deployed locations, and the establishment of OEP&P and the U.S. Forces-Afghanistan Operational Energy Division, increased priority has been given to fuel demand management initiatives at forward-deployed locations in Afghanistan. For example, DOD has undertaken a widespread initiative to replace spot generation with centralized power and the U.S. Forces-Afghanistan's Operational Energy Division secured $108 million in fiscal year 2011 from the Army to invest in more efficient power production and distribution equipment for the Afghanistan area of operations. According to DOD's analysis, this investment will remove as many as 545 spot generators saving an estimated 17.5 million gallons of fuel per year, the equivalent of removing over 7,000 fuel trucks from the roads in Afghanistan. Furthermore, the Marine Corps committed fiscal year 2011 funds to support the accelerated procurement of a suite of more efficient tactical energy systems. Also, in 2011, DOD completed the Afghanistan Micro-Grid Project,[26] which was an effort at Bagram Airfield to replace less efficient generator sets with a smart, more energy-efficient power source. DOD provided over $2 million to fund this project. Furthermore, to reinforce DOD's commitment to reducing its reliance on fuel at forward-deployed locations, in September 2011 the Under Secretary of Defense for Acquisition, Technology and Logistics issued a memorandum to support reprogramming overseas contingency operations funds to expedite the deployment of more efficient generators, centralized power projects, and shelter modification kits to forward-deployed locations in Afghanistan.[27]

---

[26]A microgrid is a power distribution system that includes multiple energy storage components, such as solar power components, or generators, which can be managed by controls depending on the power source and energy load.

[27]The Under Secretary of Defense for Acquisition, Technology and Logistics Memorandum for Commanders, U.S. Central Command, U.S. Forces Afghanistan; Subject: Operational Energy Requirements for U.S. Forces in Afghanistan; Sept.14, 2011.

With the establishment of OEP&P, DOD also has increased its efforts to obtain visibility over funding for initiatives aimed at reducing fuel consumption at forward-deployed locations. For example, to help ensure the services' budgets support the implementation of DOD's operational energy strategy, OEP&P is now required by law to publish an annual operational energy budget certification report. This report certifies that the proposed services' budgets are adequate for the implementation of the operational energy aspects of their respective energy strategies. According to OEP&P's fiscal year 2012 budget certification report, the services anticipate spending approximately $4 billion on operational energy initiatives over the next 5 years. Although the operational energy initiatives identified through OEP&P's budget certification process are not specifically targeted for use at forward-deployed locations in Afghanistan, many of them have been tested and fielded there, and will be applicable to DOD's fuel demand management efforts both in Afghanistan and elsewhere. To improve the energy efficiency of DOD's operational forces, the fiscal year 2012 President's Budget also included an additional $19 million in funding for an Operational Energy Capabilities Improvement Fund. Its mission is to fund innovation to improve operational effectiveness by investing in research and development for operational energy innovation. These funds are intended as "seed money" to consolidate or initiate promising operational energy programs. The initial funding for these efforts will be administered by OEP&P, but the programs will be ultimately sustained by the services. According to DOD, the initiatives funded by this program will support efforts to develop and rapidly transition energy technologies for the combat force, resulting in improved military capabilities, fewer energy-related casualties, and lower costs for the taxpayer. As part of this fund, in January 2012 DOD allotted funds to begin developing six new operational energy initiatives. Although these initiatives are not finalized and are still being developed, DOD expects these efforts to play a role in reducing fuel demand at forward-deployed locations. Initiatives such as the development of new energy-efficient containerized living units used in expeditionary bases around the world, energy-efficient heating and air conditioning systems, and newly designed shelter systems used to decrease fuel demand at forward-deployed locations are some of the products being developed under this program.

In addition to the initiatives mentioned above, DOD has placed a higher priority on ensuring contractors responsible for executing operations and maintenance contracts are addressing energy efficiency issues at forward-deployed locations. For instance, the U.S. Army Materiel Command[28] has taken steps to enforce the existing language included in Logistics Civil Augmentation Program (LOGCAP)[29] contracts to require more attention be given to increasing energy efficiency at forward-deployed locations. To address power generation concerns, a June 2011 LOGCAP policy letter indicates that contractors should complete assessments for the more than 4,000 generators located on over 130 bases in Afghanistan to assess power load demand and energy efficiency. The U.S. Army Materiel Command and U.S. Forces-Afghanistan also plan to include energy efficiency standards in the technical specifications for new and refurbished facilities maintained by support contractors. Further, contractors will also now be required to provide energy assessments and make recommendations for improved efficiency to supported units. According to DOD and LOGCAP officials, these and other efforts are ongoing and are expected to assist DOD in reducing its fuel consumption at forward-deployed locations. Officials also told us that by increasing efforts to reduce fuel demand, U.S. forces will both reduce operational costs associated with high fuel consumption and increase combat capability by freeing up forces used to protect fuel convoys and reduce forces' exposure to hostile action.

DOD Guidance for Fuel Demand Management

DOD has issued guidance for fuel demand management and is developing comprehensive guidance for its operational, planning, and training decisions. Since our 2009 report on fuel demand management, various DOD organizations have issued guidance for fuel demand management and the department is still developing more comprehensive guidance on how to incorporate energy efficiency considerations into DOD's operational, planning, and training decisions. In our 2009 report, we found that DOD had not developed overarching fuel demand management guidance to require commanders to manage and reduce fuel consumption at forward-deployed locations. In addition, we found that

---

[28]The U.S. Army Materiel Command is the Army's provider of materiel readiness—technology, acquisition support, materiel development, logistics power projection, and sustainment—to the total force, across the spectrum of joint military operations.

[29]The Logistics Civil Augmentation Program (LOGCAP) is an Army program that plans for the use of a private-sector contractor to support worldwide contingency operations. Examples of the types of support that may be provided under these contracts include: laundry and bath, food service, sanitation, billeting, maintenance, and power generation.

there was little or no written guidance that addressed fuel demand management or energy efficiency for base camp construction or for other business decisions such as maintenance or procurement actions. We recommended that multiple organizations within DOD develop specific guidance on fuel demand management in their areas of responsibility. DOD has since issued overarching, theater-level, and base camp construction and development guidance, but is still developing policy and doctrine to provide guidance on how energy efficiency considerations will be included in operational decisions that affect fuel demand management at forward-deployed locations, such as those in Afghanistan.

To provide overarching guidance to DOD's operational energy efforts, including reducing its reliance on fuel at forward-deployed locations, DOD published its 2011 operational energy strategy and its 2012 implementation plan. As noted above, the implementation plan provides DOD stakeholders involved in fuel demand management with a roadmap for accomplishing key tasks to reduce fuel demand. However, because OEP&P is a new organization and in the early stages of working within DOD to develop guidance and policies, DOD has yet to address how energy efficiency considerations will be incorporated into its joint doctrine,[30] which provides the principles that guide the employment of U.S. military forces in an operational environment and is essential to organizing, training, and equipping its units. DOD's *Operational Energy Strategy Implementation Plan* also acknowledges the need for additional comprehensive guidance and directs the Joint Staff and military departments to report to the Defense Operational Energy Board by the fourth quarter of fiscal year 2012 on how the strategy's goals will be reflected in policy, doctrine, and professional military education. The plan further states that the scope of this task includes examining departmental directives, instructions, field manuals, doctrine, professional military education curricula, and other relevant guidance in order to include energy efficiency considerations in its operational, planning, and training decisions.

---

[30]Joint doctrine includes the fundamental principles that guide the employment of U.S. military forces in coordinated action toward a common objective and may include terms, tactics, techniques, and procedures. Doctrine is the fundamental principles by which the military forces or elements thereof guide their actions in support of national objectives. Joint Publication 1-02, *Department of Defense Dictionary of Military and Associated Terms (As Amended Through 15 April 2012)*

Guidance for Construction and Base Camp Development Has Been Updated to Include Energy Efficiency Standards

Central Command has updated its guidance for construction and base camp development to place more emphasis on energy efficiency for contingency and permanent base camps that support missions in its area of responsibility.[31] Specifically, in 2009 we noted that some of DOD's combatant commands and military services had developed construction standards for forward-deployed locations, but our analysis showed that this existing guidance was largely silent with regard to fuel demand management and energy efficiency. Pertinent Central Command guidance in 2009 included only one reference to energy efficiency requiring that semi-permanent facilities—those facilities with a life expectancy of more than 2 years, but less than 25 years—be designed and constructed with finishes, materials, and systems selected for moderate energy efficiency. According to the guidance in effect at that time, semi-permanent construction standards were to be considered for operations expected to last more than 2 years. In 2009, we found that the temporary status of many forward-deployed locations, combined with a focus on quickly establishing the locations rather than on sustaining them, limited DOD's emphasis on constructing energy-efficient facilities. We recommended that DOD develop specific guidelines that address energy efficiency considerations in base construction. In October 2011, Central Command revised its policy for base camp construction standards to include a greater emphasis on energy efficiency. For example, the revised policy now calls for energy conservation best practices to be incorporated into all new construction that is to be environmentally controlled. Also, in an effort to reduce fuel consumption at forward-deployed locations, the policy requires all bases receiving power generation support from contingency contracting programs, such as LOGCAP, to conduct an electrical infrastructure assessment. According to Central Command officials, conducting electrical infrastructure assessments will allow base planners and commanders to determine areas where energy efficiency shortfalls may be occurring, and identify areas where energy generation and distribution adjustments should be made in order to save fuel. The policy also includes other notable provisions to promote energy efficiency such as encouraging the insulation of temporary facilities when funds and time allow. Central Command and OEP&P officials told us that revisions to this policy encourage commanders to consider incorporating energy efficiency

---

[31]U.S. Central Command Regulation 415-1, Construction and Base Camp Development in the USCENTCOM Area of Responsibility (AOR), *"The Sandbook"* Headquarters United States Central Command (Oct. 17, 2011).

standards into base camp construction and development, which may not have otherwise been an area of concern.

In addition, in April 2012, the Commander of Bagram Airfield, one of the major U.S. logistics bases in Afghanistan, issued additional guidance to direct the use of energy efficiency design and construction standards for all new and renovation construction projects on Bagram Airfield. For example, the guidance requires new or renovated projects to use energy-saving equipment such as fluorescent or Light-Emitting Diodes (LED) lighting, energy-efficient motors, and that windows, ceilings, walls, and roofs be insulated, among other things. According to an OEP&P official, all requests for approval to build or alter facilities must be reviewed by Bagram's Joint Facilities Utilization Board, which provides a way to enforce efficiency standards throughout this location.

Commanders in Afghanistan Have Recently Issued Theater-level Fuel Demand Management Guidance to Influence Maintenance and Procurement Decisions

In 2011 and 2012, commanders in Afghanistan issued theater-level fuel demand management guidance regarding maintenance and procurement decisions for forward-deployed locations. In our 2009 report on fuel demand management we found a lack of attention to fuel demand management in guidance, including an absence of fuel usage guidelines and metrics to evaluate progress of reduction efforts, as forward-deployed locations are maintained and sustained over time. We also found the procurement of products for forward-deployed locations presents opportunities for DOD to consider making purchases that take into account fuel demand or energy efficiencies when practical. Since that time, commanders in Afghanistan have issued general policy memoranda on repairing, maintaining, and procuring equipment to help reduce fuel consumption at forward-deployed locations. Specifically, in June and December of 2011 the Commander, U.S. Forces-Afghanistan, issued operational energy guidance in the form of policy memoranda[32] to soldiers, sailors, airmen, Marines, and civilians of U.S. Forces-Afghanistan located at forward-deployed locations. These memoranda stated that commanders are expected to take ownership of fuel demand management issues and explore methods for reducing fuel demand at forward-deployed locations. For example, commanders are to ensure personnel take action to repair faulty equipment, avoid using heating and air conditioning in unoccupied buildings, and work with support

---

[32] *Commander, U.S. Forces-Afghanistan policy memo, Subject: Supporting the mission with operational energy*, June 7, 2011; *Commander, U.S. Forces- Afghanistan policy memo, Subject: Supporting the mission with operational energy*, Dec. 11, 2011

contractors, suppliers, and the services to improve inefficient facilities and devices such as generators and air conditioning units. In addition, commanders should push for rapid fielding of new fuel savings methods, where appropriate, and pursue existing, proven alternative energy options that reduce the use and transport of fuel. During our visit to forward-deployed locations in Afghanistan in October 2011, however, many of the commanders and personnel we spoke with were unaware of this guidance or commented that it did not provide specific direction on how to implement needed fuel demand management actions. As such, many of the commanders with whom we spoke had not establish specific guidance or protocols to address day-to-day fuel use, such as establishing a base policy on turning off lights in unoccupied buildings or immediately repairing faulty equipment. In addition, we found that some of the commanders we spoke with in Afghanistan were not using available energy efficient equipment and/or had not fixed faulty equipment. For example, at Camp Sabalu-Harrison we observed inefficient generator configurations in which multiple generators were used to power individual tents when one generator could have provided adequate power for multiple tents (see fig. 3). At Camp Leatherneck we observed, and were told that available tent shading used to provide cover from the sun was not being used consistently throughout the base (see fig. 4).

Figure 3: Inefficient and Unnecessary Use of Multiple 60-kilowatt Generator Sets at Camp Sabalu-Harrison

Source: GAO.

Figure 4: Expeditionary Living Facilities at Camp Leatherneck without DOD-recommended Solar Shading

Source: GAO.

Additionally, at Joint Combat Outpost Pul-A-Sayed, we observed an entry control checkpoint powered by a 60-kilowatt generator when, according to the commander in charge of this outpost, a smaller more energy-efficient 5- or 10-kilowatt generator would have provided adequate power (see fig. 5). Army officials at this location told us that the previous generator used to power this entry control checkpoint had failed and had not been replaced because it was considered a lower priority. According to officials at the outpost, these types of equipment breakdowns happen frequently, and due to the lack of adequately trained personnel and other mission requirements, may take weeks to be repaired or replaced.

Figure 5: Entry Control Point at Joint Combat Outpost Pul-A-Sayed Using a More Powerful than Necessary 60-kilowatt Generator

Source: GAO.

After our visit to Afghanistan, U.S. Forces-Afghanistan developed and issued a fragmentary order[33] to provide specific guidance on fuel demand management procedures, and specific operational energy practices needed to comply with the policy memoranda. The April 2012 operational energy fragmentary order[34] established milestone dates for accomplishing tasks for reducing fuel demand at select forward-deployed locations. According to DOD officials, this type of guidance provides U.S. Forces-Afghanistan's subordinate commands with the specific direction necessary to begin reducing fuel demand at its forward-deployed locations. The order requires commanders located at forward-deployed locations in Afghanistan to distribute the December 2011 operational energy policy memo so that personnel will be aware of fuel demand management goals and objectives for forward-deployed locations. In

---

[33]A fragmentary order is an abbreviated form of an operation order issued as needed after an operation order to change or modify that order or to execute a branch or sequel to that order. When we use "order" in this section, we are referring to the fragmentary order.

[34]USFOR-A FRAGO 12-122: Directs Energy Guidance IAW USFOR-A Policy, April 2012.

GAO-12-619 Defense Energy Management

addition, the order requires commanders to develop, distribute, and implement policies that will complement the operational energy policy memorandum no later than 30 days after the order was published. Furthermore, the guidance requires that fuel accountability metrics be established and made available by U.S. Forces-Afghanistan's Joint Staff (J-4) by the end of May 2012.

Further, service officials acknowledged the need for additional training throughout the department on fuel demand management, and told us the services are developing various curricula and training programs to make sure personnel deployed to forward-deployed locations know how to operate relevant equipment and understand the importance of reducing fuel demand. For example, U.S. Marine Corps Training and Education Command has begun developing and adding operational energy courses to its expeditionary warfighting school curricula and, according to officials, has begun working with other services to further educate military personnel on the importance of energy conservation.

OEP&P officials stated that DOD's focus on operational energy issues and the organizations supporting this effort are new, and expect these efforts to have an impact on fuel demand management at forward-deployed locations as they are implemented. OEP&P officials added they are monitoring progress and will report to the congressional defense committees on operational energy management and the implementation of the operational energy strategy as required by the 2009 National Defense Authorization Act.[35]

---

[35] Pub. L. No. 110-417, § 331 (2008).

DOD has Efforts Underway to Promote Fuel Efficiency, Coordination, and Collaboration but Opportunities Exist to Enhance Efforts to Identify and Track All Fuel Demand Management Initiatives

DOD has several ongoing initiatives to promote fuel efficiency at forward-deployed locations in Afghanistan and has established various methods to facilitate some coordination and collaboration among the services. However, it is still in the process of developing a systematic approach to identify and track the numerous fuel demand management initiatives that have been fielded, or are in the research and development phase throughout DOD. Without a systematic approach, DOD may be limited in its ability to provide full visibility over all of its fuel demand management initiatives, achieve efficiencies, and avoid unintended duplication or overlap of activities.[36]

Fuel Demand Management Initiatives

We found that DOD, the services, and Central Command have numerous efforts underway to develop and test various fuel demand management initiatives. The Army and the Marine Corps have each established facilities to test fuel demand management initiatives being pursued by their respective service for potential use at forward-deployed locations. For a list of fuel demand management initiatives being evaluated by the services for possible use in Afghanistan see appendix III.

The services are engaged in several fuel demand management initiatives that can be applied to forward-deployed locations in Afghanistan. In 2011, the Army's Base Camp Integration Laboratory located at Fort Devens, Massachusetts, began assessing new systems and technology that may help increase energy efficiency and reduce fuel usage at base camp operations. The Base Camp Integration Laboratory seeks to integrate and verify new technology concepts and allows product testing before field evaluation by soldiers. According to Army officials, by conducting laboratory, systems, and interoperability testing on the items at the lab,

---

[36]Duplication occurs when two or more agencies or programs are engaged in the same activities or provide the same services to the same beneficiaries. Overlap occurs when programs that have similar goals, devise similar strategies and activities to achieve those goals, or target similar users.

the Army can improve survivability, and sustainability, and reduce the risks that may occur after new technology is deployed to the field.

Some of the specific initiatives currently being tested at the Base Camp Integration Laboratory are:

- Energy-efficient shelter testing to determine the energy efficiencies of various tent shelter alternatives.
- Soft Wall Shelter/Environmental Control Unit/Insulated Liner/Solar Shade testing to determine the effects of solar shades and insulated liners in reducing the solar load and temperature differential in soft-sided shelters. Additionally, these tests will determine if downsizing the environmental control unit can sustain interior temperatures in soft-sided shelters, thereby reducing power consumption.
- Force Provider Micro Grid testing to determine the efficiency and energy savings from replacing six generators with a microgrid within a 150-man base camp environment.

In a separate initiative to evaluate Marine Corps-specific equipment, the Marine Corps Experimental Forward Operating Base (ExFOB) was established to provide industry with an opportunity to demonstrate their latest capabilities to enhance the Marine Corps' self-sufficiency and reduce its need for bulk fuel and water at forward-deployed locations such as those in Afghanistan. To date there have been four iterations of the ExFOB. The first was conducted at Quantico, Virginia in March 2010 and involved the evaluation of, among other things, tent liners, Light-Emitting Diodes (LED) lights, soldier-portable solar recharging power devices, and a solar power energy collection and storage device. Those technologies were determined to have the potential to increase combat effectiveness by reducing the requirements for fuel and batteries, and were deployed to Afghanistan for further evaluation. The second was conducted at Twentynine Palms, California in August 2010 and evaluated hybrid solar systems, direct-current-powered efficient air conditioners, and solar power refrigerators. As a result of this ExFOB demonstration, the Marine Corps has finalized its evaluation of four items, which are now ready for use at forward-deployed locations in Afghanistan. The third ExFOB was conducted in Twentynine Palms, California in August 2011 and included an evaluation of the fuel efficiency of tactical vehicles. The fourth ExFOB was conducted at Camp Lejune, North Carolina in April and May 2012 and included an evaluation of wearable electronic power systems, lightweight, man-portable, water purification systems.

In addition, in fiscal year 2008 the U.S. Central Command and the OSD Energy Task Force cosponsored an initiative called the NetZeroPlus Joint Capabilities Technology Demonstration, an initiative used to determine fuel demand reduction solutions for forward-deployed locations.[37] This demonstration assessed technologies for reducing fuel demand and improving infrastructure and alternative energy supply for the warfighter. According to DOD officials, this demonstration used research and development efforts from military research development and engineering centers, federal and private labs, and commercial and government off-the-shelf technology. DOD plans to use the combined capabilities developed from these tests to establish more energy-efficient forward operating base blueprints for use by operational commanders, theater planners, and interagency organizations. The emphasis for this initiative was on improving or replacing current facilities with more energy-efficient structures and integrating renewable energy technologies with improved energy generation solutions to power those structures. Some of the initiatives tested as part of the technology demonstration included: air beam energy-efficient tents; power shades; solar shades; insulation liners; and flexible lighting surfaces. See appendix III for an overview of these initiatives.

Efforts Underway to Foster Coordination and Collaboration but Challenges Remain

DOD has taken some steps to foster coordination and collaboration on the department's fuel demand management initiatives, but because there are multiple organizations within DOD engaged in developing these initiatives, challenges remain. Our prior work has shown that leading practices for collaborating to meet modern national security challenges include,[38] developing and implementing overarching strategies, creating collaborative organizations, and sharing and integrating information across agencies via a comprehensive database to track initiatives. DOD has multiple organizations—including some engaged in coordination and collaboration—in the area of energy efficiency, but it currently lacks a

---

[37]A NetZero installation, over the course of a fiscal year, matches or exceeds the total electrical energy it consumes with alternative energy generated from nonfossil fuel sources.

[38]GAO, *Interagency Collaboration: Key Issues for Congressional Oversight of National Security Strategies, Organizations, Workforce, and Information Sharing*, GAO-09-904SP (Washington, D.C.: Sept. 25, 2009) and *Warfighter Support: Actions Needed to Improve Visibility and Coordination of DOD's Counter-Improvised Explosive Device Efforts*, GAO-10-95 (Washington, D.C.: Oct. 29, 2009).

formal means of sharing and integrating information across various offices engaged in these efforts.

Numerous organizations within each of the services and DOD have a role in managing, researching, and developing energy efficient technologies. See table 1 below for a list of the DOD organizations involved in fuel demand management efforts. While these organizations have different responsibilities and missions, they are each involved in fuel demand management efforts.

Table 1: DOD Organizations Involved In Fuel Demand Management Efforts for Forward-deployed Locations

Organization	Roles
Office of the Secretary of Defense	
The Assistant Secretary of Defense for Operational Energy Plans and Programs (ASD (OEP&P))	ASD (OEP&P) provides oversight of DOD's operational energy plans and programs, and is responsible for coordinating and overseeing the operational energy planning and program activities of DOD and the services, and coordinating research and development efforts related to operational energy demand and supply technologies, and monitoring and reviewing all operational energy initiatives in DOD.
The Assistant Secretary of Defense for Research and Engineering (ASD (R&E))	ASD(R&E) provides science and technology leadership throughout DOD shaping strategic direction and strengthening the research and engineering coordination efforts within the DOD community.
Defense Advanced Research Projects Agency's (DARPA)	DARPA applies multi-disciplinary approaches to both advance knowledge through basic research and create innovative technologies to address current practical problems.
Joint Committee on Tactical Shelters (JOCOTAS)	The role of the Committee is to eliminate duplication of tactical shelter research and development; maximize usage of DOD standard family of tactical shelters; and share technical & program information.
Project Manager-Mobile Electric Power (PM-MEP)	PM-MEP provides modernized, technologically advanced, tactical, diesel fueled, lightweight, portable, reliable, rugged, power generating systems in a variety of sizes.
Joint Staff	
Joint Staff for Engineering (J-4)	J-4 integrates logistics planning and execution in support of joint operations and advises the Chairman of the Joint Chiefs of Staff on logistics matters. The J-4 also serves as the primary agent of the Chairman of the Joint Chiefs of Staff for all bulk petroleum matters.
Unified and Combatant Commands	
U. S. Transportation Command	TRANSCOM provides air, land, and sea transportation for the Department of Defense, during peace and in times of war. TRANSCOM is tasked with the coordination of people and transportation assets to allow the United States to project and sustain forces, whenever and wherever they are needed. TRANSCOM also develops long-range plans for petroleum support of the inter-theater mission and contingency operations worldwide.

Organization	Roles
U. S. Central Command	U.S. Central Command promotes cooperation among nations, responds to crises, and deters or defeats aggression, and supports development and, when necessary, reconstruction in order to establish the conditions for regional security, stability, and prosperity. CENTCOM also ensures fuel support is provided to combat forces to accomplish those missions assigned by the President and the Secretary of Defense.
Defense Agencies	
Defense Logistics Agency Energy	DLA Energy's mission is to provide the Department of Defense and other government agencies with comprehensive energy solutions in the most effective and efficient manner possible. DLA meets the petroleum support requirements of the combatant commands and the military services.
Army	
U.S. Army Natick Soldier Research, Development and Engineering Center	The U.S. Army Soldier Systems Center, located in Natick, Massachusetts, researches, develops, fields, and manages food, clothing, shelters, airdrop systems, and soldier support items.
Army Base Camp Integration Laboratory (BCIL)	The BCIL is a dedicated, open architecture laboratory environment for the rapid design, development, and evaluation of advanced prototype soldier systems. The BCIL facilitates the technology maturation assessment of new technology concepts related to soldiers and allows more extensive testing than is currently possible prior to soldier field evaluation.
U.S. Army Corps of Engineers	The U.S. Army Corps of Engineers provides engineering, construction, real estate, stability operations, and environmental management products and services for the Army, Air Force, other assigned U.S. Government agencies, and foreign governments. They create and shape policy and perform strategic planning, direction, and oversight of research and development for the Corps Military and Civil Works programs, and for the warfighter. Additionally, they advise the Chief of Engineers on matters of science and technology.
The 249th Engineer Battalion (Prime Power)	Prime Power provides advice and technical assistance in all aspects of electrical power and distribution systems; and generates and distributes prime electrical power in support of Army operations worldwide.
Army Rapid Equipping Force (REF)	The REF equips operational commanders with commercial off-the-shelf and government off-the-shelf solutions to increase effectiveness and reduce risk; inserts future force technologies and surrogates to validate concepts and speed capabilities to the soldiers; and assesses Army business practices, desired capabilities, and acquisition techniques to effect institutional Army change.
U.S. Army Capabilities Integration Center (ARCIC)	The ARCIC supports the Commanding General, U. S. Army Training and Doctrine Command in the design, development, and integration of force capability requirements for the Army. The ARCIC uses wargaming, experimentation, and concepts to develop and integrate capability requirements from a comprehensive perspective of doctrine, organization, training, materiel, leadership and education, personnel, and facilities (DOTMLPF). The ARCIC also provides the management structure for identifying capability gaps and directing analytical support of DOTMLPF developments. This includes validation of research and development priorities for key Army science and technology needs, and the development and validation of integrated operational architectures depicting warfighting capabilities.
Marine Corps	
Deputy Commandant for Combat Development and Integration (DC CD&I)	The Logistics Integration Division, within DC CD&I coordinates support for combat development and requirements, and coordinates with E2O on expeditionary energy. DC/CD&I also leads training, through Training and Education Command, and doctrine development.

Organization	Roles
Marine Corps Systems Command (MCSC)	MCSC is the Commandant of the Marine Corps's agent for acquisition and sustainment of systems and equipment used to accomplish their warfighting mission.
Marine Corps Warfighting Laboratory	Marine Corps Warfighting Lab chairs the Experimental Forward Operating Base (ExFOB) Executive Integrated Process Team.
Marine Corps Expeditionary Energy Office (E2O)	The USMC E2O analyzes, develops, and directs the Marine Corps' energy strategy in order to optimize expeditionary capabilities across all warfighting functions.
Experimental Forward Operating Base Office (ExFOB)	ExFOB identifies, evaluates, and accelerates the Marine Corps' ability to increase energy efficiency as established in the Marine Corps' Expeditionary Energy Strategy and Implementation Plan.
Navy	
Navy Energy Coordination Office (NECO)	The NECO supports Task Force Energy and coordinates the overall Navy Energy strategy. Specifically, the NECO supports energy efficiency, conservation, and alternative energy investments for Navy tactical (maritime, aviation, and expeditionary) and shore forces, developing a comprehensive Navy energy strategy, and coordinating with Naval Systems Commands to ensure programs are effectively implemented.
Navy Research Laboratory (NRL)	NRL is the corporate research laboratory for the Navy and Marine Corps and conducts a broad program of scientific research, technology, and advanced development.
Air Force	
Assistant Secretary of the Air Force for Installations, Environment, and Logistics (SAF/IE)	SAF/IE shapes policy direction, conducts oversight and liaison with the Office of the Secretary of Defense, Congress, federal agencies, and external organizations. SAF/IE also provides guidance, direction, and oversight on all matters pertaining to the formulation, review, and execution of plans, policies, programs, and budgets relative to specific functional responsibilities.
Air Force Research Laboratory (AFRL)	AFRL develops and integrates affordable warfighting technologies for aerospace forces. It is a full-spectrum laboratory, responsible for planning and executing the Air Force' science and technology program. AFRL leads a worldwide government, industry and academia partnership in the discovery, development and delivery of a wide range of technology. The laboratory provides leading-edge warfighting capabilities to preserve U.S. advantages in air, space and cyberspace.

Source: DOD.

Some Collaboration and Coordination on Fuel Demand Management Initiatives Is Taking Place

Since our 2009 report on fuel demand management, DOD has taken steps to facilitate collaboration and coordinate among the services' fuel demand management efforts. In that report, we found that each of the services had efforts planned or underway to reduce fuel demand at forward-deployed locations, but lacked a systematic approach to share this information among the services. In addition, officials also reported that forward-deployed locations often pursued different initiatives, and the department, other services, or other forward-deployed locations were often unaware of these different initiatives. To address these concerns, we recommended that the services assign senior energy officials to identify and promote sharing of fuel reduction best practices and solutions to identified challenges and communicate those practices and solutions to the DOD Director of Operational Energy Plans and Programs (since renamed to be the Assistant Secretary of Defense for Operational Energy Plans and Programs) for potential use across the department.[39]

Since 2009 DOD has taken several steps to promote and facilitate coordination and collaboration in order to improve information sharing among various DOD organizations involved in fuel demand management efforts at forward-deployed locations such as those in Afghanistan. Some of these steps include the following activities:

- DOD published DOD Directive 5134.15 specifying OEP&P's responsibilities which include: coordinating and overseeing the operational energy planning and program activities of DOD and the services related to implementation of the operational energy strategy; coordinating R&D investments related to operational energy demand and supply technologies, and monitoring and reviewing all operational energy initiatives in DOD.
- DOD established some organizations such as the Defense Operational Energy Board cochaired by the Assistant Secretary of Defense (OEP&P) and the Joint Staff Director for Logistics to serve as a collaborative organization to promote operational energy security, oversee implementation of the operational energy strategy, and measure the department's success. This board will provide a forum for DOD components to share information and provide recommendations on fuel demand management initiatives.
- OEP&P in collaboration with Central Command and other DOD stakeholders sponsored an operational energy conference in May 2011 to identify operational energy problem areas and solutions. OEP&P and the Pacific Command repeated this effort in March 2012 and held an Operational Energy Summit targeting energy efficiency applications in the Pacific.
- U.S. Forces-Afghanistan established an Operational Energy Division within U.S. Forces- Afghanistan. The Operational Energy Division will assist commanders located in Afghanistan to improve operational capabilities by reducing the military's reliance on petroleum fuels. According to its charter, the Operational Energy Division will work with

[39]GAO, *Defense Management: DOD Needs to Increase Attention on Fuel Demand Management at Forward-Deployed Locations*, GAO-09-300 (Washington, D.C.: Feb. 20, 2009).

commanders develop, coordinate, and implement materiel and nonmateriel energy solutions.

- Central Command established a formal coordination body for operational energy in its area of responsibility. This organization will focus on maintaining mission effectiveness while reducing energy demand, expanding and securing energy supply, and changing the culture through energy awareness. Membership and supporting agencies include a wide range of leaders throughout DOD and the service components assigned to Central Command's area of responsibility.

In addition, the services continue to use several collaborative organizations that predate the establishment of OEP&P to coordinate and collaborate on their fuel demand reduction efforts including those that are applicable to forward-deployed locations. For example:

- Program Manager for Mobile Electric Power. This program, established in 1967, was created to consolidate research and development efforts, establish common military operational requirements, and prevent duplication in the development of equipment such as generators that are used to supply power at forward-deployed locations. This effort has resulted in the development of a new energy-efficient family of generators called Advanced Medium Mobile Power Source (AMMPS) to be used by both Army and Marine Corps units. AMMPS includes Army and Marine Corps specifications and according to DOD officials, is a good example of how coordination and collaboration can help DOD accomplish its goals in a more cost-effective manner while still meeting the unique needs of each service.
- The Joint Committee on Tactical Shelters. This committee was created in 1975 to prevent the duplication of tactical shelter research and development efforts. According to DOD, since its establishment, this committee has reduced the number of shelter types from 100 to 21 easing the logistics burden among the four services. Collaboration through this committee has allowed DOD to limit the number of shelter systems developed to decrease fuel consumption at forward-deployed locations.
- Other collaborative forums. The USMC-SOCOM board, Army-Marine Corps board, and the Power Source Technical Working Group, all provide a means to coordinate and communicate on initiatives such as fuel demand management efforts. According to DOD officials, these collaborative forums take place at least twice a year and help the services discuss and share information related to issues such as fuel demand management and other programs of mutual interest.

DOD Lacks Information Sharing Mechanisms for Systematically Identifying and Tracking Fuel Demand Management Initiatives

DOD has established multiple organizations and forums to facilitate coordination and collaboration, but does not have a mechanism to systematically identify and track information on the numerous fuel demand management initiatives that have been fielded, or are in the research and development phase throughout DOD. For instance, in an attempt to identify a list of fuel demand management initiatives, we sent a request to OEP&P asking for a comprehensive list of initiatives that had been fielded or were expected to be fielded to forward-deployed locations in Afghanistan within the next 12 months. [40] OEP&P officials could not provide us with a comprehensive list of initiatives at the time of our request, and told us they did not have a mechanism in place to track or catalog all ongoing fuel demand management initiatives. In order for us to obtain a comprehensive list of initiatives an OEP&P official told us they would have to query all of the services and agencies involved to obtain this type of information.

Both DOD's experience and our prior work have shown the benefits of enhanced information sharing for increasing coordination and collaboration, especially when multiple entities are involved in similar efforts. [41] For example, our prior work has shown that identifying and tracking specific detailed program information can enhance visibility and oversight efforts, and provide decision makers with timely and comprehensive information needed to determine management priorities. Moreover, OEP&P's directive outlining its roles and responsibilities states that OEP&P will recommend appropriate funding levels for operational energy programs relating to the operational energy strategy.

The Joint Committee on Tactical Shelters and the Program Manager for Mobile Electric Power demonstrate how increased collaboration on fuel demand management initiatives can improve interoperability among systems, consolidate research and development efforts, save life-cycle costs, all while meeting the unique needs of each service. In addition, our prior work on other DOD management issues found that establishing a database to identify and track information could enhance DOD's ability to

---

[40]Information requested from OEP&P was asked for in November 2011; 12 months from the time of the request would be November 2012.

[41]GAO, *Warfighter Support: Actions Needed to Improve Visibility and Coordination of DOD's Counter-Improvised Explosive Device Efforts*, GAO-10-95 (Washington, D.C.: Oct. 29, 2009); and *Defense Acquisitions: Opportunities Exists to Improve DOD's Oversight of Power Source Investments*, GAO-11-113 (Washington, D.C.: Dec. 30, 2010).

improve program management, visibility, and avoid investing in duplicative efforts. According to an OEP&P official, the number of initiatives and organizations involved in DOD's efforts to reduce its reliance on fuel has increased, and oversight and continued efforts to coordinate and collaborate across DOD are necessary. During our visit to forward-deployed locations in Afghanistan, Army officials also reiterated that frequently the various DOD organizations involved in developing fuel demand management solutions are unaware of ongoing efforts and establishing a mechanism to increase DOD's visibility to identify all ongoing fuel demand management efforts would be useful.

Since OEP&P did not have a mechanism in place to catalog fuel demand management initiatives underway within DOD, we queried the services and various DOD organizations to collect data on the initiatives being pursued within DOD.[42] Based on the information they provided, we identified over 30 initiatives being developed by the services and other DOD organizations to reduce DOD's fuel demand at forward-deployed locations. (See app. III for the list of initiatives). Additionally, during our visit to the U.S. Army Soldier Systems Center in Natick, Massachusetts,[43] officials told us that although our review was limited to fuel demand management initiatives for base camps at forward-deployed locations in Afghanistan, DOD had numerous projects aimed at reducing fuel demand at forward-deployed locations around the world, but at the time of our visit no office or organization was tracking all of these initiatives.[44] An official with the Office of the Assistant Secretary of Defense for Research and Engineering ASD(R&E) involved in identifying operational energy investments and initiatives confirmed that ASD(R&E) was not tracking

---

[42]These operational energy initiatives include those being developed to reduce fuel consumption in expeditionary environments, including at forward-deployed locations in Afghanistan.

[43]The U.S. Army Soldier Systems Center, located in Natick, Massachusetts researches, develops, fields, and manages food, clothing, shelters, airdrop systems, and soldier support items.

[44]Initiatives mentioned by Natick officials, include efforts such as developing alternative fuel types, redesigning aircraft to achieve greater fuel efficiency, and developing electric powered tanks and trucks.

GAO-12-619 Defense Energy Management

such initiatives and relied upon the services to coordinate and manage these issues.[45]

According to DOD officials, at the time of our request, OEP&P did not have a mechanism in place to systematically track initiatives because its responsibilities are to develop and influence policy and provide guidance, oversight, and coordination of DOD's operational energy efforts and they are not involved in the services' decisions about how to equip the forces with specific energy efficiency technologies. As such, officials told us that they had not developed a systematic approach for identifying and tracking fuel demand management initiatives. Since our request, officials told us that OEP&P has started working with DOD's Office of Cost Assessment and Program Evaluation to develop an automated budget exhibit that captures detailed program and funding data on operational energy initiatives included in DOD and the component's budgets. OEP&P is in the process of refining this exhibit to capture improvements suggested by the components. This budget exhibit with consolidated information on operational energy initiatives funded in the fiscal year 2013 President's Budget submission will help the office in its oversight and coordination role, but OEP&P officials acknowledge that its effort has a knowledge gap. For example, it does not include information on initiatives that are the subject of rapid fielding efforts or are locally procured. OEP&P officials stated that the Operational Energy Division in Afghanistan has started to collect information on ongoing operational energy activities in theater. However, these efforts have just begun and it is unclear to what extent they will provide a comprehensive list of all operational energy initiatives underway within DOD. As mentioned earlier, over the next 5 years, the services plan to spend approximately $4 billion dollars on operational energy initiatives, and without an established mechanism to identify and track fuel demand management initiatives, DOD may miss opportunities to improve its return on investment, reduce life-cycle costs, consolidate efforts, and increase interoperability among fuel demand management technologies.

---

[45]Office of the Assistant Secretary of Defense for Research and Engineering ASD(R&E) has been tasked in the implementation plan with assessing current science and technology investments and initiatives across the department, operational energy needs and requirements, and new technical opportunities, including from outside DOD.

DOD Has Measured the Results of Some Fuel Demand Management Initiatives, and Is Developing Baseline Data to Assess Progress Toward Achieving Operational Energy Goals

DOD has measured the results of some of the fuel demand management initiatives used in Afghanistan, but only recently has focused on collecting and assessing the data needed to develop a comprehensive baseline measure of its current fuel consumption at forward-deployed locations. Recognizing the need for information to manage fuel demand effectively, DOD has tasked the services with establishing baselines for operational energy consumption in all activities (air, sea, land) in its March 2012 implementation plan and provided funding for this purpose. Once collected, this baseline data will provide information across DOD's operational activities, including those conducted in Afghanistan, and help the department better understand how specific assets consume fuel in an operational environment.

Service Efforts to Measure the Results of Some Fuel Demand Management Initiatives Are in the Early Stages and Face Some Challenges

As noted above, DOD has developed fuel demand management initiatives, and has begun, in some cases to measure their results. However, the services are still in the process of collecting and analyzing comprehensive baseline data for all activities—to include fuel consumption at forward-deployed locations in Afghanistan—and have encountered some implementation challenges. In 2011, DOD issued guidance that emphasizes the importance of collecting data to assess progress and program effectiveness. Both DOD's strategic management plan and its operational energy strategy highlight the importance of collecting and analyzing data for use in assessing and managing performance of its initiatives. Specifically, DOD's strategic management plan states that one of its business goals is to increase operational energy efficiency in order to lower risks to warfighters, reduce costs, and improve energy security. To help achieve this goal, the plan calls for establishing an operational energy baseline for the department that is based on credible, verifiable fuel usage data. Furthermore, the operational energy strategy states that a greater understanding of how energy is used will allow DOD to target investments to improve energy efficiency in places such as Afghanistan. Recognizing the lack of sufficient data to manage fuel demand effectively, the Army and Marine Corps, which have the largest presence at forward-deployed locations in Afghanistan, have begun to collect fuel use and behavior data to understand how equipment is being used in combat to inform decision making on how to best employ equipment in the future.[46]

The Army Has Begun Efforts to Measure Fuel Consumption

At the time of our report, the Army had begun collecting and analyzing data on particular fuel demand management initiatives and on its current fuel consumption at forward-deployed locations in Afghanistan. However, its data collection efforts face some continuing challenges. Among its ongoing fuel demand management initiatives, the Army has collected preliminary fuel consumption data on its new Advanced Medium Mobile Power Source (AMMPS) generators (see fig. 6). According to Army officials, replacing 273 Tactical Quiet Generators in Afghanistan with AMMPS generators is estimated to save about 1,100 gallons of fuel per day.[47] Furthermore, in August 2011, the Army installed a 1-megawatt microgrid at Bagram Airfield that replaced 13 60-kilowatt Tactical Quiet Generators (see fig. 7). The Army collected data from the microgrid to analyze its fuel consumption and identified a savings of 7,344 gallons of fuel (17 percent), over the test period.[48] The Army's February 2012 report of the microgrid concluded that producing energy can be done more efficiently if the Army understands how the energy will be used. It stated that without these types of data, the Army is currently running generators inefficiently in the field, which places a burden on logistical operations. According to the report, by using information such as forecasted scenarios and energy demand, the department can weigh the trade-offs and implement a system with optimum efficiency.

---

[46]Forward operating bases in Afghanistan are managed by the ground component, which consists largely of Army and Marine Corps forces. Although outside the scope of our review, the Air Force and Navy also have efforts underway to measure fuel consumption.

[47]Army officials provided these data based on preliminary testing of AMMPS generators that were run on full-load conditions and assumes the generators were run 24 hours per day.

[48]The U.S. Army Materiel Systems Analysis Activity office collected data from the microgrid from August-November 2011 to independently analyze its fuel consumption and compared it to the baseline data they collected on the 13 Tactical Quiet Generators that the microgrid replaced.

Figure 6: Advanced Medium Mobile Power Source (AMMPS)

These generators use advanced technologies to improve power generation capability and improve engine control to achieve greater fuel efficiency. Modeling and testing have been conducted to determine how the generators perform under different energy loads.

Status: 273 AMMPS will be sent to Afghanistan in spring of 2012 with about 1200 more expected to be deployed in 2013.

Source: Program Manager for Mobile Electric Power.

Figure 7: 1-megawatt Microgrid at Bagram Airfield

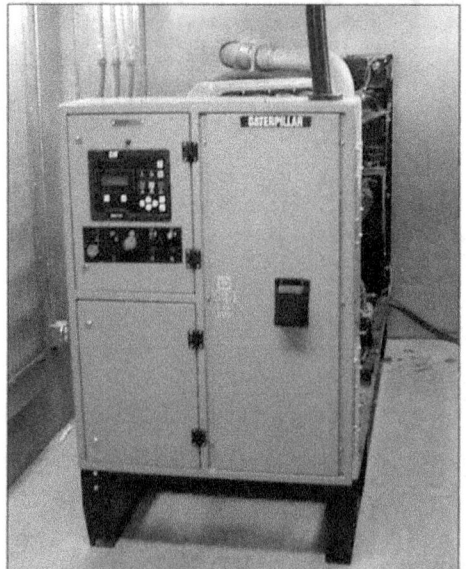

This system of power generating components actively matches supply capacity to demanded load with the goal of saving fossil fuel in austere environments. Data collection and analysis have been conducted on the microgrid.

Status: Deployed at Bagram Air Field since August 2011.

Source: Program Manager for Mobile Electric Power.

The Army has also begun measuring fuel consumption by testing initiatives at its Base Camp Integration Laboratory at Fort Devens, Massachusetts, an initiative mentioned earlier to test and evaluate fuel demand management equipment (see fig. 8). The goal of the Base Camp Integration Lab is also to assess fuel consumption of equipment traditionally used at forward operating bases such as those in Afghanistan, and fuel consumed by new technology concepts and prototypes.

Figure 8: Aerial shot of the Base Camp Integration Laboratory at Fort Devens, MA

Source: U.S. Army.

As of October 2011, Army officials stated that the Base Camp Integration Laboratory had completed baseline testing and had begun testing the energy efficiency of various shelters, as well as a microgrid. Army officials stated that future testing will be conducted on insulated tent liners, a photovoltaic system incorporated in a microgrid, and a solar-powered water heater.

The Marine Corps Has Begun Efforts to Measure Fuel Consumption

As discussed above, the Marine Corps has developed operational energy initiatives, including those to decrease fuel demand, and also has begun measuring the results of some of these initiatives, primarily those that serve battalion-sized units. As noted above, the Marine Corps established the Experimental Forward Operating Base (ExFOB) in 2009 to bring stakeholders together across the service's requirements, acquisitions, and technology communities to inform requirements and rapidly evaluate new technologies for potential deployment. The four ExFOB demonstrations conducted thus far have evaluated initiatives such as renewable energy power generation, tent liners, hybrid solar systems, more efficient air conditioners, and solar-powered refrigerators. After evaluation, infantry battalions deployed to Afghanistan with selected equipment items to further assess their performance. A Marine Corps' assessment[49] found that during deployment:

- two platoon positions were able to run completely on renewable energy for 1 month,
- one patrol base was able to save 175 gallons of fuel in a 1-month period by utilizing the ExFOB initiatives,
- the Green Renewable Expeditionary Energy Network System (GREENS) provided full power for a platoon guard station, and
- Marines were able to reduce the number of batteries they had to carry by using the Solar Portable Alternatives Communications Energy System (SPACES) to recharge tactical batteries.

Challenges Remain in Measuring Current Fuel Consumption

The Army and Marine Corps face challenges in collecting information on current fuel consumption at forward-deployed locations in Afghanistan. Until recently, information related to fuel demand in-theater has been available only in the form of sales receipts and fuel delivery summaries, since DOD only tracks the movement and delivery of fuel up to the point that a forward-deployed location receives it, and as indicated above, efforts to collect current fuel consumption data face challenges. As a result, DOD lacks comprehensive data on how much fuel specific assets such as generators and air conditioning units consume in an operational environment. The Army and Marine Corps have begun collecting information on fuel consumption at their forward-deployed locations in Afghanistan. For this effort Army and Marine Corps officials told us that both services are using the Tactical Fuels Manager Defense system technology (see fig. 9). To date, the Tactical Fuels Manager Defense system has been deployed to 36 locations in Afghanistan. Army officials stated that the information gathered by this system can assist a base commander in making decisions regarding energy use on the base, but they indicated that this technology is not yet being used at all forward-deployed locations and cited several difficulties they face.

---

[49]The Marine Corps Operational Test and Evaluation Activity Forward Operations Afghanistan team deployed to Afghanistan to assess the use of various initiatives by a battalion in-theater after being evaluated at the ExFOB. This assessment of the initiatives used in theater did not include an evaluation of transport vehicles such as trucks, tanks, and humvees used for military operations in Afghanistan.

Figure 9: Tactical Fuels Manager Defense System

Source: DOD.

An Army software system that provides accountability and enterprise-wide visibility of fuel down to the retail level. The system can incorporate handheld devices to scan barcodes affixed to individual assets, such as generators or vehicles, to automate the collection of fuel consumption data by an individual asset.

For instance, additional funding will be required to extend the Tactical Fuels Manager Defense system to the majority of locations in Afghanistan. In addition, during our site visit to forward-deployed locations in Afghanistan, officials reported that they had experienced difficulty in connecting to the system's website, which resulted in an inability to load fuel data points, receipts, and stock levels into the system. In addition to these technical challenges, the program manager stated that additional training and oversight procedures were needed to ensure soldiers and Marines use this system and are held accountable for importing data. For example, the program manager told us that some bases are not entering fuel consumption data into the system and from September 2011 to March 2012, the data captured had declined by 50 percent making it more difficult for DOD to meet its goal in obtaining baseline fuel data. In response, the International Security Assistance Force Joint Command

GAO-12-619 Defense Energy Management

issued a fragmentary order in April 2012 specifically to ensure all bases follow existing accountability and reporting procedures, including using the Tactical Fuels Manager Defense system to capture fuel data. While the system is providing improved data on fuel consumption at forward-deployed locations, Army officials also recognize that continued evaluation and improvements will be needed before deciding whether this should be an Army-wide system.

DOD Has Begun Collecting Baseline Data to Assess Effectiveness of Its Fuel Demand Management Efforts

While the services have efforts underway to obtain a better understanding of how specific assets consume fuel in-theater, DOD has limited ability to assess the effectiveness of its fuel demand management initiatives because it has only recently begun efforts to collect comprehensive baseline data across the services. DOD recognizes the need for baseline data on fuel consumption in an operational environment and has taken several steps to address this issue. Specifically, OEP&P's implementation plan tasks the services with establishing operational energy consumption baselines and projecting consumption for fiscal years 2012—2017[50] by the second quarter of fiscal year 2012. DOD's implementation plan states that these projections will inform required reports to Congress on current and future energy needs. In addition, the implementation plan calls for the services to report to the Defense Operational Energy Board by the third quarter of fiscal year 2012 on any actions taken or needed to improve these baselines. The plan states that this effort may not necessarily entail the real-time measurement of energy consumption by individual pieces of equipment. Instead, the military departments and defense agencies may evaluate a range of options—including new systems, improvements to current and related systems, and/or application of sampling and extrapolation to existing data—to improve the department's understanding of the location, purpose, and end use of operational energy consumption. This implementation plan is an important step towards improving the department's management of its energy consumption at forward-deployed locations such as those in Afghanistan; however, the focus on establishing a baseline of fuel consumption is relatively recent.

---

[50]According to the implementation plan, the data collected for fiscal year 2011 will account for consumption by military forces as well as consumption by contractors. The estimated consumption for fiscal years 2012-2017 will use assumptions about inventory, equipment, and operations tempo using agreed-upon scenarios.

GAO-12-619 Defense Energy Management

In addition, U.S. Forces-Afghanistan is in the process of improving their visibility and accountability over fuel consumption at forward-deployed locations. To help with this task, OSD officials informed us that DLA-Energy sent an analyst to Afghanistan in March 2012 to work with the U.S. Forces-Afghanistan's Operational Energy Division to capture a better picture of fuel consumption.[51] Officials stated that with improved visibility, they expect that the Operational Energy Division will be able to articulate to combatant commanders or service officials the costs associated with certain operational decisions and leverage this improved picture of fuel consumption to target areas for improvement.

Further, to support fuel demand management efforts at forward-deployed locations, OEP&P provided additional funding for a demonstration effort to evaluate the operational benefits of fuel demand management. Specifically, DOD provided $1.4 million to fund the Operation Enduring Freedom Energy Initiative Proving Ground to evaluate initiatives including heat and air conditioning units, tent liners, solar tent shades, and hybrid-solar electrical power technology, and analyze the effect these initiatives have on fuel consumption and identify opportunities to deploy them in Afghanistan to achieve the greatest impact and return on investment. The group in charge of this effort has already begun to take inventory of the power and energy used at some forward-deployed locations and to monitor areas where there are opportunities for potential energy efficiency improvements.

Conclusions

In its extended war in Afghanistan, DOD reports that its heavy reliance on petroleum-based fuel at forward-deployed locations continues to create risk for the warfighters, pose difficult logistical challenges for military planners, and increase the department's operating costs. With consistent and heightened visibility from Congress and OSD, DOD has made progress in its efforts to develop an approach for managing its fuel demand at forward-deployed locations since the time of our 2009 report on this issue. The creation of the Assistant Secretary of Defense for Operational Energy Plans and Programs and the services' operational energy offices, OEP&P's publication of its operational energy strategy and implementation plan, the services' strategies, and the ongoing fuel

---

[51]DLA-Energy is the integrated materiel manager for class III bulk fuels and shares responsibility over Afghanistan with the North Atlantic Treaty Organization's Joint Forces Command.

demand management initiatives the services have deployed or are developing all represent positive steps toward reducing the department's reliance on petroleum-based fuel at forward-deployed locations such as those in Afghanistan. DOD's efforts to develop specific guidance on how military forces should factor operational energy considerations into its operational, planning, and training decisions are important steps toward minimizing key problems identified by DOD—risk to warfighters, logistical-related disruptions, and high operating costs—associated with heavy reliance on petroleum-based fuel. However, without a mechanism for systematically collecting and sharing information across the services on the fuel demand management initiatives that have been fielded, or are in the research and development phase, DOD may forgo an opportunity to improve interoperability of new technologies, consolidate research and development efforts, and save costs. Lastly, DOD's recent efforts to begin collecting accurate baseline data on fuel demand at the individual asset level at forward-deployed locations should enhance its planning, programming, and operational decisions, and help measure the impact of its fuel demand management efforts as well as progress toward meeting its overall operational energy goals. At a time when the federal government faces increasing fiscal challenges and competition across the government for discretionary funds, these efforts by DOD could help maximize the benefits of its energy efficiency investments for forward-deployed locations and better position the department for future missions.

Recommendation for Executive Action

To further enhance DOD's approach for managing fuel demand, including at forward deployed locations such as those in Afghanistan, we recommend that the Secretary of Defense direct the Assistant Secretary of Defense for Operational Energy Plans and Programs, in consultation with the Joint Staff, combatant commanders, and military service components, to finalize and implement a systematic approach that includes establishing a mechanism to identify and track fuel demand management initiatives that have been fielded, or are in the research and development phase to ensure information concerning these efforts is effectively shared across the services.

Agency Comments and Our Evaluation

We provided a draft of this report to DOD for comment. In its written comments, reproduced in appendix IV, DOD partially concurred with our recommendation to finalize and implement a systematic approach that includes establishing a mechanism to identify and track fuel demand management initiatives that have been fielded, or are in the research and development phase to ensure information concerning these efforts is effectively shared across the services. DOD also provided technical comments that were incorporated, as appropriate.

DOD stated that it signed the DOD *Operational Energy Strategy Implementation Plan* in March 2012 and established the Defense Operational Energy Board with the purpose of providing a mechanism for reviewing, synchronizing, and supporting departmentwide operational energy policies, plans, and programs. DOD also stated that the Defense Operational Energy Board's membership ensures departmentwide coordination. Furthermore, DOD stated that the *Operational Energy Implementation Plan* addresses energy improvements in current operations, and the Board will oversee the tracking and sharing of information on fuel demand improvements. Lastly, DOD stated that the department conducts an annual review of the components' budgets and activities to determine their adequacy for implementing the *Operational Energy Strategy*, and this review also encompasses fuel demand management initiatives that are being developed, fielded, or supported by the budget. As such, DOD stated that while our recommendation has merit, further action by the Secretary of Defense is unnecessary.

We acknowledge the intended actions described in DOD's *Operational Energy Strategy Implementation Plan*, the function and scope of the Defense Operational Energy Board, and DOD's annual review process, which may eventually provide DOD with an approach and mechanism for identifying and tracking fuel demand management initiatives that have been fielded, or are in the research and development phase. However, until these initiatives are fully implemented, we are unable to assess the extent to which they will address our recommendation. During the course of our review, DOD officials explained that many of the initiatives included in its *Operational Energy Strategy Implementation Plan*, such as identifying investment gaps in the department's science and technology portfolio necessary to reduce fuel demand, would be completed at the end of fiscal year 2012 or beyond. DOD officials also told us they were in the process of finalizing the department's annual review of the components' budgets and activities to include fuel demand management initiatives that were being developed or fielded. However, at the conclusion of our review, this budget review process had not been finalized and the department acknowledges that its annual budget review efforts do not include initiatives that are part of rapid fielding or are locally procured. We continue to believe that a comprehensive mechanism for sharing information on all initiatives underway within the department, including those that are part of rapid fielding or are locally procured, would further enhance DOD's approach for managing fuel demand at forward-deployed locations such as those in Afghanistan, and help ensure information concerning these efforts is effectively shared across the services.

We are sending copies of this report to the appropriate congressional committees. We are also sending copies to the Secretary of Defense. In addition, the report is available at no charge on the GAO website at http://www.gao.gov.

If you or your staff have questions about this report, please contact me at merrittz@gao.gov or (202) 512-5257. Contact points for our Offices of Congressional Relations and Public Affairs may be found on the last page of this report. GAO staff who made key contributions to this report are listed in appendix V.

Zina D. Merritt
Director
Defense Capabilities and Management

Appendix I: Scope and Methodology

Our objectives were to assess the extent to which DOD has (1) established an approach to provide visibility and accountability for fuel demand management at forward-deployed locations, (2) initiatives underway to promote fuel efficiency across the services in Afghanistan and has facilitated coordination and collaboration among the services on the development and fielding of these initiatives, and (3) measured the results of its fuel demand management initiatives at forward-deployed locations. To gather information for these objectives, we reviewed documentation and interviewed officials from:

Office of the Secretary of Defense

- Office of the Assistant Secretary of Defense for Operational Energy Plans and Programs
- Office of the Assistant Secretary of Defense for Research and Engineering

Joint Staff

- J-4 Logistics Directorate, Engineering Division

U.S. Army

- Deputy Assistant Secretary of the Army (Energy and Sustainability Office)
- Army G-4
- Army Corps of Engineers
- 249th Prime Power Battalion
- Army Rapid Equipping Force
- Army Petroleum Center
- Program Manager Mobile Electric Power
- Green Warrior Initiative; Contingency Basing & Operational Energy
- Natick Solider Research, Development, Engineering Command
- Logistics Civil Augmentation Program

U.S. Navy

- Deputy Assistant of Secretary of the Navy, Energy Office
- Navy Energy Coordination Office

U.S. Air Force

- Air Force Office of the Assistant Secretary, Installation, Environment, and Logistics
- Air Mobility Command Fuel Efficiency Office

U.S. Marine Corps

- Marine Corps Expeditionary Energy Office
- Marine Corps Systems Command
- Marine Corps Training and Education Command

U.S. Central Command

- U.S. Forces Afghanistan-Operational Energy Division
- New Kabul Compound
- Camp Phoenix
- Camp Sabalu-Harrison
- Joint Combat Outpost Pul-A-Sayed
- Camp Leatherneck,
- Patrol Base Boldak,
- Bagram Airfield.

Defense Agencies

- Defense Logistics Agency – Energy

We concentrated our review on the steps the Army and Marine Corps have taken to reduce fuel demand because these two services have the responsibility for managing forward-deployed locations in Afghanistan. Our review focused on fuel demand management initiatives planned for or underway at forward-deployed locations in Afghanistan. For the purposes of our review, we defined fuel demand management initiatives to include nonmateriel and materiel solutions to assist DOD in reducing its reliance on fuel consumed at forward-deployed locations. We did not examine energy efficiency initiatives for naval vessels, aircraft, or combat vehicles. We asked officials to identify key initiatives planned or under way to reduce fuel demand. After consultation with U.S. Central Command and U.S. Forces Afghanistan officials, we selected and visited forward-deployed locations because they were using energy-efficient technologies that were included in our review and/or are illustrative of DOD's fuel demand management initiatives and challenges. The locations chosen are illustrative case studies in our report and information obtained from these locations is not generalizable to all forward-deployed locations. We also reviewed DOD guidance related to energy reduction for the department's permanent or U.S. facilities.

To address the first objective, we identified DOD's approach for fuel demand management from our prior work examining DOD's fuel demand management efforts at forward-deployed locations.[1] These elements include: (1) establishing visibility and accountability for achieving fuel reduction by assigning roles and responsibilities, establishing metrics, and monitoring performance; (2) issuing guidance and policies that address fuel demand at forward-deployed locations; and (3) establishing incentives and a viable funding mechanism to support the implementation of fuel demand reduction projects. We reviewed DOD and Service guidance, operational energy strategies and plans, OEP&P's budget certification report, project status reports, and briefings to identify DOD's approach for fuel demand management. We also interviewed OSD, Joint Staff, service, and U.S. Central Command officials at the headquarters and operational level to discuss DOD's fuel demand management approach, and to determine the extent to which DOD has implemented the initiatives contained in its operational energy strategy. We also met with officials responsible for administering the Logistics Civil Augmentation Program contracts to discuss how energy efficiency guidance and requirements were being incorporated into contracts to incentivize fuel demand management efforts. Furthermore, we met with OEP&P, Joint Staff, and service officials to discuss the processes and steps needed to ensure an effective approach was established to provide oversight and accountability for fuel demand management and the anticipated time frames for accomplishing fuel demand management goals.

To determine the extent to which DOD has initiatives underway to manage fuel demand across the services in Afghanistan and has facilitated coordination and collaboration, we queried OEP&P, the services, and various DOD organizations involved in operational energy research and development to collect data on the initiatives to reduce fuel demand at forward-deployed locations. These initiatives included ones that had been fielded or were expected to be fielded within 12 months of our data request.[2] Based on the information provided and the scope of

---

[1]GAO, *Defense Management: DOD Needs to Increase Attention on Fuel Demand Management at Forward-Deployed Locations*, GAO-09-300 (Washington, D.C.: Feb. 20, 2009).

[2]Information was requested in November 2011; 12 months from the time of the request would have been November 2012.

our review, we identified over 30 fuel demand management initiatives already fielded or being developed by the services and other DOD organizations to reduce DOD's fuel demand at forward-deployed locations. We also reviewed data on the current status of initiatives that were identified in our 2009 report.[3] In addition, we met with Army and Marine Corps officials located at the headquarters level and at forward-deployed locations to discuss the purpose and function of these initiatives, as well as any opportunities for greater coordination and collaboration. To determine the extent to which the department has efforts underway to facilitate coordination and collaboration among the services, we conducted an analysis of DOD energy strategies and plans, reviewed DOD energy conference summary reports, attended DOD energy symposia, and interviewed DOD and service officials. Additionally, we reviewed relevant DOD, Joint, and service policies and guidance, and assessed the extent to which the policies and guidance were consistent with leading practices for coordination and collaboration identified in our prior work.[4] We also met with DOD and research and development officials to discuss the challenges, if any, that they faced to coordinate and collaborate on fuel demand management initiatives.

To determine the extent to which DOD has efforts in place to accurately capture the results of its fuel demand management initiatives in forward-deployed locations, we assessed DOD and the services' strategies that detail their goals and methods for measuring the results of their fuel demand management initiatives, and determined whether these plans addressed key elements from leading practices for measuring results (e.g. goals, milestones, quantifiable metrics, evaluation of benefits, etc.).[5] In addition, we interviewed DOD and service officials regarding the extent to which fuel demand management initiatives are being measured at forward-deployed locations in Afghanistan. The Army and Marine Corps have the largest presence at forward-deployed locations in Afghanistan, and therefore have been testing most of the initiatives. As such, we relied

---

[3]GAO, *Defense Management: DOD Needs to Increase Attention on Fuel Demand Management at Forward-Deployed Locations,* GAO-09-300 (Washington, D.C.: Feb. 20, 2009).

[4]GAO, *Results-Oriented Government: Practices That Can Help Enhance and Sustain Collaboration among Federal Agencies,* GAO-06-15 (Washington, D.C.: Oct. 21, 2005).

[5]Executive Order 13514, "*Federal Leadership in Environmental, Energy, and Economic Performance*" (Oct. 5, 2009).

on documents provided to us by DOD and the services regarding the initiatives and the results from testing their performance. We reviewed select DOD studies that assessed various initiatives being used in Afghanistan with the goal of reducing fuel use at forward-deployed locations. We concluded that the studies clearly describe the methodology and assumptions behind the study results, and they do not attempt to generalize the results beyond the context of the studies. Although the results of these studies cannot be generalized to all fuel demand management initiatives, they provide examples of how DOD is assessing the results of these initiatives. We also conducted interviews with DOD and service officials to obtain information regarding DOD's progress in collecting fuel data on fuel demand management initiatives and establishing a baseline on fuel demand at forward-deployed locations in Afghanistan.

We conducted this performance audit from April 2011 through June 2012 in accordance with generally accepted government auditing standards. Those standards require that we plan and perform the audit to obtain sufficient, appropriate evidence to provide a reasonable basis for our findings and conclusions based on our audit objectives. We believe that the evidence obtained provides a reasonable basis for our findings and conclusions based on our audit objectives.

Appendix II: Key Tasks and Milestones Included in DOD's Operational Energy Strategy Implementation Plan

Milestone	Task	Description
2nd Quarter fiscal year 2012	Develop a Charter that Outlines the Organization, Governance, Membership, Functions, and Responsibilities of the Defense Operational Energy Board	ASD(OEPP), in consultation with relevant offices within OSD, the Military Departments, Defense agencies, and the Joint Staff, will present the charter at the meeting of the Board.
2nd Quarter fiscal year 2012	Establish Operational Energy Consumption Baselines	The Military Departments and Defense agencies will report to the Defense Operational Energy Board an operational energy baseline, using all available data on actual energy consumption in support of military operations in fiscal year 2011 and projected consumption in fiscal year 2012 – 2017.
3rd Quarter fiscal year 2012	Support Current Operations with Energy Improvements	Combatant Commands will report to the Defense Operational Energy Board on how they guide their forces to improve energy performance and efficiency in operations and the effectiveness of this guidance.
3rd Quarter fiscal year 2012	Improve the Operational Energy Efficiency of the Military Departments	The Military Departments will report to the Defense Operational Energy Board progress against their own current or updated energy performance goals and metrics and demonstrate how such progress supports the Operational Energy Strategy priority to reduce the demand for fuel and increase capability in military operations.
3rd Quarter fiscal year 2012	Include Operational Energy in the Requirements Process	In accordance with forthcoming Joint Staff policy, the Joint Staff, U.S. Special Operations Command (USSOCOM), and the Military Departments will meet the congressional intent of an energy performance attribute in the requirements development process. Through the Joint Requirements Oversight Council, the Vice Chairman of the Joint Chiefs of Staff (VCJCS) will oversee implementation of this effort in individual programs. The Joint Staff, USSOCOM, and the Military Departments will report overall progress in implementing an energy performance attribute to the Defense Operational Energy Board.
3rd Quarter fiscal year 2012	Apply Operational Energy Analyses to Defense Acquisitions	In accordance with forthcoming policy from the Under Secretary of Defense for Acquisition, Technology and Logistics (USD(AT&L)), the Military Departments will develop and apply Fully Burdened Cost of Energy (FBCE) analyses throughout the acquisition process. The Military Departments will report overall progress on implementing FBCE to the Defense Operational Energy Board.

Milestone	Task	Description
3rd Quarter fiscal year 2012 & recurring	Identify Operational Energy Security Risks at Fixed Installations	The Military Departments and other asset owners will brief the Defense Operational Energy Board on energy-related risks to fixed installations that directly support military operations, to include those identified through Assistant Secretary of Defense for Homeland Defense and America's Security Affairs' (ASD(HD&ASA)) Defense Critical Infrastructure Program (DCIP).
4th Quarter fiscal year 2012	Assess Departmental Energy Science and Technology Gaps and Recommend Options	The Assistant Secretary of Defense for Research and Engineering (ASD(R&E)) will identify investment gaps in the Department's science and technology portfolio necessary to reduce demand, improve system efficiency, and expand supply alternatives, as articulated in the Operational Energy Strategy. ASD(R&E) will provide the final report to the Defense Operational Energy Board and include recommendations on possible options for filling the gaps.
4th Quarter fiscal year 2012	Adapt and Adopt Policy, Doctrine, and Professional Military Education for Operational Energy	The Joint Staff and Military Departments will report to the Defense Operational Energy Board on how policy, doctrine, and professional military education (PME) will support reduced energy demand, expanded energy supply, and future force development.
4th Quarter fiscal year 2012	Incorporate Operational Energy into Combatant Command Activities	As appropriate and consistent with annual classified guidance to the Combatant Commands, the Joint Staff and Combatant Commands will report to the Defense Operational Energy Board on command measures to incorporate Operational Energy Strategy goals into theater campaign plans, security cooperation initiatives, joint and combined exercises, and other activities designed to achieve theater and country objectives.

Source: DOD Operational Energy Strategy Implementation Plan

Appendix III: Fuel Demand Management Initiatives for Forward-Deployed Locations Identified by DOD

The list of fuel demand management initiatives included below provides an overview of the materiel initiatives identified by DOD organizations during the course of our review. This list does not include the nonmateriel initiatives underway such as those to change policies and procedures, or modify staffing to perform fuel demand management functions. The list also provides a status update on the initiatives discussed in our 2009 report on fuel demand management. The first nine initiatives listed below were identified in our 2009 report.

		Description/Status update
Initiatives identified in GAO's 2009 report		
1.	Eskimo Spray Foam Insulation	An application of foam insulation on tent structures to decrease fuel demand. According to Army officials, spray foam reduces power use for heating, ventilation, and air conditioning.
		CURRENT STATUS: The effort to insulate tents with spray polyurethane foam has been suspended. Even though the tent insulation effort was demonstrated in-theater with successful results, the Army is no longer moving forward with a large- scale effort to install foam insulation in all tents and portable structures while it examines the environmental implications of disposal of the solidified tent foam when the life span of the tent is complete.
2.	Advanced Medium Mobile Electric Power (AMMPS)	The AMMPS, a replacement for the Tactical Quiet Generators (TQGs). It takes advantage of current technology to provide power generation capabilities that are more fuel efficient and reduce overall costs.
		CURRENT STATUS: The Army is currently procuring AMMPS generators and will field them throughout the service. Some Army units will take the AMMPS with them when they deploy to Afghanistan in the future. Also, Program Manager-Mobile Electric Power is fielding approximately 200 AMMPS to Afghanistan starting in 2012 to replace legacy tactical quiet generators (TQGs). Once in place, the DOD expects AMMPS can save as much as 300,000 gallons of fuel per month over the TQGs they are replacing.
3.	Improved-Environmental Control Unit (I-ECU)	The I-ECU is a replacement of military standard environmental control units. It is designed for military environments, with reduced power consumption and weight, and increased reliability over current environmental control units.
		CURRENT STATUS: Program Manager for Mobile Electric Power (PM-MEP) begins low-rate initial production of the I-ECU in fiscal year 2012.
4.	Tactical Garbage to Energy Refinery (TGER)	An experimental device that converts trash (paper, plastic, cardboard, and food waste) into energy for forward-deployed locations, reducing the need for convoys to deliver fuel and haul away trash.
		CURRENT STATUS: TGER has been successfully tested and full system integration is underway. The Army is now targeting a field demonstration starting in mid-June for 90 days. The original destination was Bagram, but now more likely will be Camp Virginia, Kuwait.
5.	Scrap Tire Recycling Process	The scrap tire recycling process produces diesel, gas, carbon char, and steel—byproducts that can either be used to power generators, boilers, and other items or recycled into products such as asphalt and paint.
		CURRENT STATUS: This effort no longer has research investment, and is not a product being further developed.

		Description/Status update
6.	Hybrid Electric Power Station	A hybrid generator system that uses wind and solar energy to supplement diesel generators. **CURRENT STATUS:** Due to issues regarding usability the system was dismantled and disposed of in early fiscal year 2011.
7.	Transportable Hybrid Electric Power Stations (THEPS)	The THEPS are mobile generators with solar panels, wind turbine, diesel generator, and storage batteries. **CURRENT STATUS:** The Transportable Hybrid Electric Power Station was not successful but spurred the Defense Advanced Research Projects Agency to allocate $30 million to the Army to develop the Hybrid Intelligent Power (HIPower) system, a micro grid system.
8.	Monolithic Dome	This is a concrete, dome-shaped structure that is designed to be energy efficient with energy supplied by a combination of solar panels and windmills. **CURRENT STATUS:** Although successful, using domes in-theater would require some changes in current operations, as domes would be considered permanent structures and thus subject to MILCON constraints.
9.	Renewable Tent City	A collection of various deployable shelters powered by solar and fuel cell generators. **CURRENT STATUS:** There have been no Renewable Energy Tent Cities fielded in Afghanistan by the Air Force, but Air Force Central has fielded a number of sets elsewhere in-theater. The Air Force purchased and shipped a total of 920 units (flys and inserts) for the CENTCOM AOR, for Air Force training sites, and for storage at Holloman Air Force Base. Air Force Central received a total of 575 units and the majority are in use at Manas and Ali Al Salem. Units were also sent to Air Force sites for training.
Initiatives identified after 2009		
10.	Deployable Renewable Energy Alternative Module	This module is intended to be towed by a vehicle and is designed to be used at combat posts in forward-deployed locations to power equipment via solar, wind turbine, battery, and generator technologies.
11.	Smart and Green Energy (SAGE)	SAGE is an integrated effort to develop design specifications for base camp infrastructure that when employed will reduce the quantity of petroleum fuel required for electrical power generation for expeditionary camps by employing smart Micro-grid technologies and energy efficient modular structures.
12.	Rucksack-Enhanced Portable Power System (REPPS)	The REPPS is a lightweight, portable power system capable of recharging batteries and/or acting as a continuous power source.
13.	Afghanistan Microgrid Project (AMP)	The AMP initiative involves the operation of load sensing monitors and fuel consumption logs, which are being captured by the Army Materiel Systems Analysis Activity team and will be analyzed to quantify the impact of the microgrid on fuel consumption against the baseline of 13 TQGs that the system is replacing.
14.	Solar Portable Alternative Communication Energy System (SPACES)	SPACES is a lightweight man-portable lightweight device with tailorable adaptors that can energize equipment such as radios, laptop computers, and rechargeable batteries.
15.	Ground Renewable Expeditionary Energy Network System (GREENS)	GREENS is a man-transportable device with renewable energy collection and storage that can energize communications equipment, sensors, and radios.
16.	Energy at Remote Locations (EARLCON)	EARLCON is hybrid power system, using solar, traditional generators, and battery storage, with an energy management system. It is designed to improve efficiency and reduce demand for fuel.
17.	SunDanzer Direct Current powered Air-Conditioners (DCAC)	The SunDanzer direct current powered air cooler is an air conditioning system that features a variable speed compressor. This design allows for low energy consumption and the ability to connect directly to a photovoltaic array without the need for batteries.

	Description/Status update
18. Integrated Trailer Environmental Control Units (ECU) Generator	The Integrated Trailer-ECU-Generator II is a self-contained, highly mobile power generation and environmental control system. It is a second generation system of the current Integrated Trailer ECU Generator.
19. Solar Stik Hybrid Energy System-Energy to the Edge	Energy to the Edge focuses on meeting energy and water requirements at locations that are hard to support logistically, while simultaneously reducing dependence on ground and aerial resupply operations. This is a 30-kilowatt hybrid energy system designed to integrate renewable energy with the Army's currently fielded Tactical Quiet Generators.
20. Tent, Extendable, Modular, Personnel (TEMPER) Photovoltaic Fly	The TEMPER air-supported tent photovoltaic fly provides supplemental power generation without increasing the operational footprint of the base camp.
21. Solar Shade Tent Fly with Integral Photovoltaic Power	This solar shade tent fly has integrated photovoltaic power and can reduce solar load up to 80-90 percent.
22. ZeroBase H-Series ReGenerator	The ZeroBase H-Series ReGenerator is a hybrid system that has solar generation, battery storage, and a 5-kilowatt generator. The system maximizes generator efficiency by operating the generator at peak efficiencies by capturing excess power through the battery bank.
23. Mobile Max Pure System	Mobile Max Pure System is a commercial, off-the-shelf system that provides over 3 kilowatts of photovoltaic power but also integrates water pumping and purification systems as options.
24. Reusing Existing Natural Energy Wind and Solar (RENEWS)	The RENEWS system consists of wind turbines, flexible solar panels, a battery module, and output adapter plugs/connectors.
25. Insulating Liners	The Insulating Liner is a lightweight, radiant, reflective insulating liner. It is installed behind the existing liner to enhance the radiant and insulating capability, which reduces both heating and cooling requirements / needs. The Insulating liner has zippered doors and sealable openings for ducts and electrical cords to enter the shelter. These liners fit different shelter systems and provide varying levels of insulation.
26. SunDanzer Refrigerators	SunDanzer refrigerators and freezers have exceptionally low energy consumption and require smaller, less expensive power systems and low operating expense. This technology allows refrigeration in remote locations where it was previously unavailable or prohibitively expensive.
27. Battlefield Renewable Integrated Tactical Energy System (BRITES)	BRITES is an Air Force power system that stores energy and serves as a power management distribution system.
28. Alaska Small Shelter System	The Alaska Small Shelter System is the official Air Force shelter system and the only shelter successfully tested to meet all the requirements, such as wind and snow load, of the U.S. Air Force's 1999 Operational Requirements Document.
29. Utilis Thermal Fly	The Utilis Thermal Fly is an external solar shade used to reduce the severe radiant heat transfer from the outside environment to the inside of the shelter.
30. Atomic Force Photovoltaic Microscopy (Flexible Solar Cells Technique)	Flexible Solar Cells Technique works by scanning a nanoscale stylus across an array of microscopic solar cells which causes them to illuminate with simulated light so that they function. These flexible solar cells are plastic-based, and work via photovoltaic properties of the plastic, which convert a portion of the light that hits the solar cells into electricity.
31. Alternative Energy Fuel Cell Generator	This generator is in development and will be designed to be a portable, integrated, and ruggedized, polymer electrolyte membrane-based fuel cell, power generator, capable of operating on certain raw fuel. This generator will produce 10 kilowatts peak power output that is suitable for deployment to forward operating locations.
32. Solar Integrated Power Shelter System	This shelter system uses lightweight, flexible solar panels to cool a tent shelter. It is currently undergoing field testing and will be deployed initially in Kuwait in fiscal year 2013.

	Description/Status update
33. Rigid Wall Energy Efficient Shelters	These are lightweight, deployable, rigid-wall, and thermally insulated shelters that can be used as part of various fielding options.
34. L'Garde Cell Insulation	This cellular insulation project leverages NASA's multilayer film insulation concept resulting in flat panels that when mechanically deployed provide energy.
35. Balance of Systems	Balance of Systems is designed for multiple applications, including Quadrant, Temper Fly, and PowerShade. This system consists of a charge controller, power monitor, AC inverter, and two storage batteries. The power is generated by the photovoltaics flows to the charge controller, which then uses that power to charge the batteries if they are depleted.
36. Shower Water Reuse System	This shower system is designed to improve the energy, water, and waste efficiency and reduce environmental risks of life support areas.
37. Skycam power (alternative power for senor)	This initiative is an extended solar-power solution to operate a wireless surveillance system for combat outpost force protection.
38. Pinwheel (generator and solar PV)	This is an energy and power initiative that includes a generator and solar photovoltaics.
39. Hunter Defense Technologies (HDT) Heat Shield Radiant Blanket	The HDT Heat Shield Radiant Blanket is a 114-pound liner designed to help thermally insulate a Base-X tent. The HDT liner fits inside of the tent by attaching the liner to the walls and ceiling.

Source: GAO analysis of DOD data.

OFFICE OF ASSISTANT SECRETARY OF DEFENSE
3700 DEFENSE PENTAGON
WASHINGTON, DC 20301-3700

OPERATIONAL ENERGY
PLANS AND PROGRAMS

June 19, 2012

Ms. Zina D. Merritt
Director, Defense Capabilities and Management
U.S. Government Accountability Office
441 G Street, N.W.
Washington, DC 20548

Dear Ms. Merritt:

This is the Department of Defense (DoD) response to the GAO Draft Report, GAO-12-619, "DEFENSE MANAGEMENT: Steps Taken to Better Manage Fuel Demand but Additional Information Sharing Mechanisms Are Needed," dated May 25, 2012 (GAO Code 351613). The enclosed document contains comments about the draft report's recommendation.

The Department appreciates the opportunity to provide you with this response and looks forward to working with you as we continue to reduce operational fuel demand.

Sincerely,

Sharon Burke

Enclosure:
As stated

GAO Draft Report Dated May 25, 2012
GAO-12-619 (GAO CODE 351613)

"DEFENSE MANAGEMENT: STEPS TAKEN TO BETTER MANAGE FUEL
DEMAND BUT ADDITIONAL INFORMATION SHARING MECHANISMS ARE
NEEDED"

DEPARTMENT OF DEFENSE COMMENTS
TO THE GAO RECOMMENDATION

RECOMMENDATION 1: To further enhance DOD's approach for managing fuel demand, including at forward deployed locations such as those in Afghanistan, we recommend that the Secretary of Defense direct the Assistant Secretary of Defense for Operational Energy Plans and Programs, in consultation with the Joint Staff, combatant commanders, and military service components, to finalize and implement a systematic approach that includes establishing a mechanism to identify and track fuel demand management initiatives that have been fielded, or are in the research and development phase to ensure information concerning these efforts are effectively shared across the services.

DoD Response: DoD partially concurs with the recommendation. The Secretary of Defense signed the DoD Operational Energy Strategy Implementation Plan in March 2012 and established the Defense Operational Energy Board with the express purpose of providing a "mechanism for reviewing, synchronizing, and supporting Department-wide operational energy policies, plans, and programs." The Board's comprehensive membership (co-chaired by the ASD(OEPP) and the Director for Logistics, Joint Staff; with participation by OSD, Joint Staff, Military Departments, and Combatant Commands) already ensures Department-wide coordination. Second, the Implementation Plan specifically addresses energy improvements in current operations, and the Board will oversee the tracking and sharing of information on fuel demand improvements. Finally, the Department conducts an annual review of the Components' budgets and activities to determine their adequacy for implementing the Operational Energy Strategy. This annual, DoD-wide review encompasses fuel demand management initiatives that are being developed, fielded, or supported by the budget. The Department's final report is openly available to DoD personnel and offices. For these reasons DoD believes that while the GAO's recommendation has merit, further action by the Secretary of Defense is unnecessary.

Appendix V: GAO Contact and Staff Acknowledgments

GAO Contact	Zina D. Merritt, (202) 512- 5257 or merrittz@gao.gov
Staff Acknowledgments	In addition to the contact named above, Suzanne Wren (Assistant Director), Virginia Chanley, Carole Coffey, Mark Dowling, Jason Jackson, Tamiya Lunsford, Christopher Mulkins, Charles Perdue, Amie Steele, Erik Wilkins-McKee, and Delia P. Zee made major contributions to this report.

Related GAO Products

Defense Acquisitions: Opportunities Exist to Improve DOD's Oversight of Power Source Investments. GAO-11-113. Washington, D.C.: December 30, 2010.

Defense Management: Increased Attention on Fuel Demand Management at DOD's Forward-Deployed Locations Could Reduce Operational Risks and Costs. GAO-09-388T. Washington, D.C.: March 3, 2009.

Defense Management: DOD Needs to Increase Attention on Fuel Demand Management at Forward-Deployed Location. GAO-09-300. Washington, D.C.: February 20, 2009.

Defense Management: Overarching Organizational Framework Needed to Guide and Oversee Energy Reduction Efforts for Military Operations. GAO-08-426. Washington, D.C: March 13, 2008.